SKINNY Spices ™

Erica Levy Klein

SURREY BOOKS
230 East Ohio Street
Suite 120
Chicago, Illinois 60611

SKINNY SPICES is published by Surrey Books, Inc., 230 E. Ohio Street, Suite 120, Chicago, IL 60611.

This book is manufactured in the United States of America.

First edition. 2 3 4 5

Library of Congress Cataloging-in-Publication Data:

Klein, Erica Levy.
   Skinny spices: 50 nifty homemade spice blends that can make any diet delicious / by Erica Levy Klein.
   204 p.   cm.
   Includes bibliographical references. Includes index.
   ISBN 0-940625-24-5 : $8.95
   1. Spices.   2. Cookery.   I. Title.
TX819.A1K58 1991
641.6'383—dc20   90-48079
                                                 CIP

Editorial Production: *Bookcrafters, Inc., Chicago*
Cover design and art direction: *Hughes & Co., Chicago*
Illustrations: *Elizabeth Allen*

Single copies may be ordered by sending check or money order for $11.45 (includes postage and handling) per book to Surrey Books at the above address. For volume discounts or customization, contact Surrey Books. The Surrey Books catalog is also available from the publisher free of charge.

This title is distributed to the trade by Publishers Group West.

For Susanna Bensinger

"I end where I began
and know the place for the first time."
—Walt Whitman

Good Health Books from Surrey

The Free and Equal® Cookbook by Carole Kruppa
From appetizers to desserts, these 150-plus, *sugar-free* recipes will make your mouth water and your family ask for more! Make great dishes like cioppino, Caesar salad, shrimp Louisiana, stuffed peppers, and chicken cacciatore, yet keep control of calories, cholesterol, fat, and sodium. Calorie counts and diabetic exchanges.

The Free and Equal® Dessert Cookbook by Carole Kruppa
Make cheesecake, black bottom pie, chocolate bon bons, cookies, cakes—in all, 160 *sugar-free* desserts. Calorie counts and diabetic exchanges.

Skinny Soups by Ruth Glick and Nancy Baggett
More than 100 delicious, hearty, calorie-wise soups from elegant crab and mushroom bisque to exotic Malaysian chicken scallion to chilled soups and standbys such as French onion, chicken-rice, and New England fish chowder. Recipes keep careful control of fat, sodium, and cholesterol. Complete nutritional data.

The Microwave Diabetes Cookbook by Betty Marks
More than 130 delicious, time-saving *sugar-free* recipes for everyone concerned with heart-health, and especially those with diabetes. Everything from appetizers to desserts, vichyssoise to pizza. Complete nutritional data and diabetic exchanges.

Thinner Dinners in Half the Time by Carole Kruppa
Make your own diet dishes—such as Mediterranean artichoke dip, roast pork chops Calypso, chicken Veronique, and marinated salmon with pasta—then freeze ahead to keep your fridge filled with fast fixings. Over 160 delicious time-savers.

The Restaurant Companion: A Guide to Healthier Eating Out
by Hope Warshaw, M.M.Sc., R.D.
All the practical information you need to order low-cal, low-fat, high-nutrition meals in 15 popular cuisines! Includes ethnic restaurants, fast-food chains, even airlines.

Skinny Spices by Erica Levy Klein
50 nifty homemade spice blends, ranging from Ha Cha chili to Moroccan mint, to make even diet meals exciting! Spice blends require no cooking and add *zero* fat, cholesterol, or calories to food. Includes 100 recipes.

The Love Your Heart Low Cholesterol Cookbook by Carole Kruppa
250 low-cholesterol recipes for everything from appetizers to desserts. Enjoy the great tastes—with *no* cholesterol—of deviled eggs, Italian bean soup, oriental chicken salad, chocolate cake, and many more easy-to-make delights. Complete nutritional data.

Feeding Your Baby: From Conception to Age 2 by Louise Lambert-Lagacé
First U.S. edition. Complete information on good nutrition for babies—and mothers—before, during, and after pregnancy. Includes breast-feeding (with tips for working moms), advice on formulas, how to introduce solids, recipes for homemade baby foods, dealing with problem eaters, and much more.

Acknowledgments

Special thanks to Susan Schwartz and Margaret Liddiard of Surrey Books for their publishing smarts and enthusiastic belief that *Skinny Spices* represented a healthy eating trend whose time had come. To Barry Mizes, for his conscientious recipe evaluations and review. And most of all, to my husband, Ken Kroll, who never cared about my weight and made me feel beautiful no matter what the scale said.

Contents

Introduction

If I have one quarrel with diet books, it's that the author always portrays herself (or himself) as an example of dieting perfection and implies the rest of us can only experience the same success if we embrace the author's particular eating and fitness regimen. Have you ever noticed how they never seem to endorse anyone *else's* diet and fitness plan? I guess there's just too much ego (and too many dollars) on the line to expect an author to be that objective.

I hope you'll find this a refreshing change of pace, but I refuse to pretend that my Skinny Spice blends are the miracle weight loss cure the world has been waiting for. You can coat yourself in curry powder, dunk yourself in dill, or submerse yourself in cinnamon and you'll still weigh exactly the same unless you're ready to make permanent changes in the way you eat, the way you think about food, and the way you exercise. Making this three-part commitment to a different lifestyle is essential—otherwise you'll just lose the pounds temporarily and gain them all back when you return to eating "normally."

You can take my word for this unfortunate fact. I started out a 215-pound teenager, lost 70 pounds with physician-prescribed diet pills, ate myself back up to 180, Weight Watchered down to 140, high-anxietied up to 185, and then finally lost 55 pounds on Nutri-System (which takes a more behavioral approach to weight loss) and have been a comfortable 130 pounds ever since.

The good news is that spices (and especially the delicious spice blends described in this book) can be a real boon to your weight-loss efforts whether you're trying to slim down on your own or have joined an organized program such as Nutri-System, Weight Watchers, Diet Center,

Weight Loss Center, or Jenny Craig. Some of the sweeter blends can even liven up liquid-based diets such as Optifast* and what I call the "poor man's" version—Slim Fast and Ultra Slim Fast.

Why are spices and herbs such excellent diet aids? Because they add next to no calories, fat, or salt to foods, whether they're used individually or in combination. But even more importantly, spices and herbs can make an *incredible flavor difference* in foods that are the staples of any low-calorie diet. I'm talking about the foods that strike fear in every dieter's heart (and stomach)—chicken and turkey . . . fish . . . cottage cheese . . . unbuttered vegetables . . . plain boiled, broiled, and steamed dishes . . . and unsweetened desserts. In short, the foods we usually burn out on long before our weight-loss goals are ever achieved.

With a flavor boost from a *Skinny Spices* homemade spice blend, even low-calorie, low-sodium, low-fat foods can taste more interesting and satisfying. Suddenly, diet choices can go from being punishments (foods to be suffered through and endured) to meals you can actually savor, enjoy, and *live with*—which is one of the real secrets of controlling your weight. And you don't have to cook them; mixing or grinding is all that's necessary.

Just for the record, spices don't have to be "hot" or "tongue tingling." Spices can be cool like my Delicious Dill Blend . . . rich like my Butter Baby Blend . . . sweet like my Choc-o-holic Blend . . . nutty like my Open Sesame Blend . . . or fragrant like my Garlic & Ginger Blend. Just think of them as a miniature "flavor fix" whenever you want to liven up a food you wouldn't normally be able to even look at one more time—much less eat.

Even recent research studies confirm that spice blends like Skinny Spices are a dieter's best friend. A recent study from Canada shows that when you eat a tasty, palatable meal, you burn more calories than eating exactly the same meal in a less flavorful form. Scientists speculate that the sight, smell, and taste of foods we like stimulate our bodies to burn significantly more calories than when we're faced with bland, boring, or unappetizing foods. Still another

*Consult a doctor before adding any ingredient to Optifast or any other physician-prescribed liquid diet formula.

study, this one from Japan, shows that by including more capsaicin (the "red hot" in red pepper) in your food, you may be able to fight obesity by increasing your metabolic rate.

Skinny Spices is the first book that looks at spice blends exclusively as a diet aid. It contains more than 50 fast, easy-to-prepare recipes for blends of spices and herbs that will produce mouthwatering gourmet dishes from appetizers and entrees to sweet treats and desserts. I've deliberately kept the spice blends simple (and cooking-free) and the recipes that use them even simpler. That way you can experiment on your own without investing a lot of time and effort in the kitchen. (Frankly, if I see a recipe that has more than five steps, I just flip the page.)

Furthermore, all recipes in *Skinny Spices* have been tested and reviewed for accuracy, then computer-analyzed for calorie, fat, sodium, and cholesterol counts. With a *Skinny Spices* recipe, you always know exactly what you're eating and can then decide how you want to work the dish into your individual diet plan.

As an added bonus, *Skinny Spices* includes tips on mail order sources for both typical and hard-to-find spices, suggestions for handy spice-related gadgets and gizmos, and a list of my favorite brand-name substitutes for high-calorie foods that can help satisfy cravings when you just can't live without that slice of cheesecake or apple pie but don't want the guilt or the calories of the real thing.

I'd enjoy getting your feedback about *Skinny Spices,* and you can feel free to write to me in care of the publisher with your questions or comments. In the meantime, I wish you a healthy life that proves "a little spice is always nice."

ERICA LEVY KLEIN

5,000 Years of Spicy History

Get ready for everything you always wanted to know about spices from the dawn of civilization to the present day. And all in 15 seconds or less!

Spices have always been considered a valuable commodity, and archaeological evidence suggests that spices in one form or another have been selling at a brisk clip for the past 5,000 years. The Egyptians were the first to recognize the value of spices and use them as aromatics and perfumes. Later, when spices became the method of choice for food preservation, their sea-going cousins, the Phoenicians, traded spices for salt and tin along Europe's Mediterranean coast. But it was really the Arabs who were the most successful in opening up spice trading routes throughout the Muslim and Roman empires, and in a relatively short amount of time (historically speaking), they dominated the world's spice trade.

After the fall of Rome, the Venetians took their turn at trying to gain control of the world's highly lucrative spice trade routes. But eventually even these merchants of Venice found themselves sharing their routes with ships from Portugal, Spain, Holland, and England.

The plantations that eventually sprang up as a result in colonies throughout the New World assured that spices were no longer controlled by any one country. Today, spices arrive in our supermarkets and gourmet shops from every part of the tropics, and demand is so high that spices are often the mainstay of an entire country's economy.

Did you get all that? Great! There'll be a quiz on Monday. But in the meantime, you've just earned an honorary DOS degree—Doctorate of Spice-ology!

4

Getting the Skinny on Skinny Spices

Are Skinny Spices really all that skinny when it comes to calories? Happily, the answer is yes. Most spices and seasonings weigh in at between 3 and 10 calories a level teaspoon, according to the American Spice Trade Association. (C'mon, would they lie, I ask you?)

Since most recipes require only ⅛ to ½ teaspoon of a particular spice or spice blend, and that amount is usually divided among six or eight portions, you can quickly see why spices are a dieter's best friend. Spices are also incredibly low in fat, protein, carbohydrates, and sodium, making them ideal for medically restricted or special diets.

Here's a brief overview of calorie counts for various spices:

- Seasonings with 5 calories or less per teaspoon:

basil	rosemary
bay leaf	sage
garlic powder	savory
marjoram	tarragon
parsley flakes	thyme

- Seasonings with 6 to 10 calories per teaspoon:

allspice	coriander
caraway seed	cumin
cardamon	dill
cinnamon	fennel
clove	ginger

mace
dry mustard
onion powder
oregano

paprika
pepper, all types
sesame seeds
turmeric

- Seasonings with under 15 calories per teaspoon:

celery seeds
nutmeg
poppy seeds

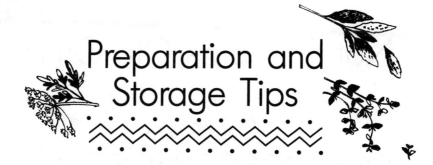

Preparation and Storage Tips

One beauty of the spice blends that follow is that you just have to mix them—no cooking is necessary. It's that simple! But to bring out the best in your spices, try these helpful tips, courtesy of Barbara Gibbons, "The Slim Gourmet." Barbara is also the author of *Light and Spicy*, a marvelous low-calorie, spice cookbook:

- Try marinating or heating herbs in oil to bring out their deepest flavors.
- Enhance the flavor of seeds such as poppy and sesame by toasting in a regular oven or toaster oven.
- Keep spices in a cool, clean, dry place out of the sunlight to prevent evaporation of oils and flavor.
- Keep containers tightly closed after each use.
- Use ground spices within a year to take advantage of best flavor. (Whole spices keep their flavor almost indefinitely and may be purchased in larger amounts.) Herbs tend to lose flavor a little faster than spices, so you may want to use them up sooner.
- To preserve herbs, either freeze or dry them. Before either process, wash and dry herbs well. *To freeze:* spread in a single layer on a baking sheet in the freezer. After herbs are completely frozen, pack them up in small freezer bags. Use frozen herbs in soups, stews, and hot dishes or defrost for use in salads and cold foods. *To dry:* in the microwave, lay herbs on a sheet of paper toweling and cook for several minutes on high. In the oven, scatter herbs on a baking sheet in a slow oven with the door open, watching carefully to see that they don't get crisp.

Not the Same Old Grind: Spicy Gadgets & Gizmos

Depending on the ingredients in a *Skinny Spices* blend (and whether you prefer powdery or coarsely ground spice blends), you may want to process your herbs and spices for a few seconds in a *blender, coffee grinder,* or *food processor.* Of course, you can also resort to the old fashioned method and use a *mortar and pestle* along with plenty of elbow grease. But lazy spice blender that I am, I always prefer to use a high-tech timesaver.

These days, I use a *blender* to achieve the consistency I want with many of my own homemade blends—especially combinations that contain peppercorns, nutmeg, stick cinnamon, or whole coriander. If you don't happen to own a blender, grinder or processor, you can crush these spices by placing them between two sheets of wax paper (or in a baggie) and flattening them with a rolling pin. However, a blender offers an added advantage in that it can uniformly mix a spice blend in a way that's difficult to achieve any other way.

I've also had great success with the Pepper Mate, an all white, space-age pepper mill that looks like a child's oversized wind-up toy. A special acrylic compartment at the bottom of the device catches the freshly ground spices. Another good alternative is the hand-held spice grinder set from The Spice Merchant, a mail order firm that specializes in Asian spices, condiments, and foodstuffs. The set includes six empty jars, each with its

8

own grinder and acrylic storage container. The Spice Merchant's address is listed in the "Your Mail Order Guide to Spices" in the back of the book, but I'll also repeat it here:

The Spice Merchant
P.O. Box 524
Jackson Hole, WY 83001
(307) 733-7811

Another alternative to these techniques is to use a *food processor,* but generally, you're compelled to make bigger batches of the spice blend before this appliance is really effective, and it's dangerously easy to overprocess and turn your spice blend into a spice paste. Although this is not a major disaster, *Skinny Spice* blends are simply more distinctive—and more eye-appealing—when the spices retain their original form.

All of the spices and herbs used in the following recipes are in their dried form. If you want to use fresh equivalents, the ratio is ⅓ to ½ teaspoon of dried = 1 tablespoon of fresh. It's best to begin with more conservative amounts of herbs and spices and add more according to your taste.

Spices from A to Z

Imagine yourself strolling slowly through a fragrant garden filled with every spice and herb from around the world and this is just a sample of what you'd find:

allspice—its scent reminiscent of cinnamon, cloves, and nutmeg, "all" rolled into one.

anise—a sweet, licorice-like taste that's terrific with vegetables, stews, and soups.

basil—sweet and pungent; great in tomato sauce or combined with oregano and garlic in Italian dishes.

bay leaf—a strong taste that stands up to poultry, fish, sauces, and stews.

caraway—with a mild, tangy quality that's similar to dill seed.

cardamon—sharp, pungent, and sweet with a cinnamon-like aroma.

cayenne pepper—a tongue-searing red pepper that adds a lively kick to "tame" foods.

celery seed—celery-like flavor that zips up tuna, coleslaw, and salad dressings.

chervil leaf—a strong, herbal taste with just a hint of tarragon. The perfect complement for fish, vegetables, and salads.

chives—the mild onion taste that's wonderful heaped generously onto salads, soups, and plain-baked potatoes.

cilantro—dried coriander leaf with an exotic parsley-like flavor that livens up poultry, vegetables, and sauces.

cinnamon—sweet, fragrant, and versatile enough to spice up everything from desserts and drinks to beef and chicken.

cloves—a type of evergreen bud typically found in spiced drinks, marinades, glazes, and sweet treats.

coriander—spicy and citrus-like. Great for chili, stir-frys, and coleslaw.

cumin—the major flavor ingredient in most chili powders. Especially good on meats and in yogurt-based dishes.

dill weed—the feathery leaf of the dill plant, with a pungent kick and a light, heady fragrance.

fennel seed—sweet, licorice-like seeds similar to anise but a lot milder in taste. A lovely addition to pork, fish, or seafood dishes.

fenugreek—spicy, slightly bitter maple-like flavor that is usually found in curry mixtures.

garlic—adds a dazzling, pungent flavor and fragrance to any dish. New varieties will even leave your breath smelling sweet!

ginger—a sharp, spicy-sweet fragrance that's perfect for adding a taste of the Orient.

horseradish—a white root with a hot, hearty flavor.

mace—the ground outer covering of nutmeg, with a more compelling, pungent fragrance.

marjoram—a milder cousin of oregano.

mint—light, fragrant, and comforting. Peppermint is the more biting variety; spearmint is a lot milder.

mustard—hot and spicy; a devilish addition to salad dressings, eggs, and vegetable dishes.

nutmeg—mild, nutty, distinctive, and fragrant. Great in sweets or in sauces.

oregano—the dominant herb in many spaghetti sauces, and just as terrific with tomatoes, peppers, zucchini, eggplant, and dips.

paprika—a mild, ground reddish pepper that's delicious with chicken, eggs, and dressings.

parsley—the ever-present garnish, with an herbal flavor that's great in soups, stews, sauces, and salad dressings.

pepper—a spicy berry found in three familiar forms: black, green, and white.

poppy seed—tiny seeds with a sweetish, nutty taste and texture.

rosemary—fragrant, strongly flavored leaf that looks like a miniature pine needle. The ultimate herb for chicken.

saffron—the most expensive of all spices, a traditional accompaniment to many Indian, Spanish, and Mediterranean dishes.

sage—strong, pleasant flavor with a sweet, herbal fragrance.

savory—a mild, thyme-like taste that adds special fragrance to meats and fish.

sesame seed—mild, nut-like flavor and a pleasant, toasted quality.

tarragon leaf—a rich, sweet flavor and fragrance faintly reminiscent of anise.

thyme—distinctive, pleasant herbal flavor and fragrance that's wonderful with seafood, tomato-based sauces, or in salad dressings.

turmeric—a brilliant yellow ground spice with a peppery aroma and a ginger-like flavor. Adds the golden color to curry powder.

A Quick Guide to Helpful Measurements and Sweetener Equivalents

- **General Measurements**

3 teaspoons	= 1 Tablespoon
1 Tablespoon	= ½ fluid ounce
4 Tablespoons	= ¼ cup
8 Tablespoons	= ½ cup
1 cup	= ½ pint
2 cups	= 1 pint
4 cups	= 1 quart
4 quarts	= 1 gallon
8 ounces	= ½ pound
16 ounces	= 1 pound

- **Dry Sweetener Approximate* Equivalents**

1 packet	= 2 teaspoons sugar
3 packets	= 2 Tablespoons sugar
6 packets	= ¼ cup sugar
12 packets	= ½ cup sugar
25 packets	= 1 full cup sugar

*Most sweeteners vary in sweetness according to the brand. For best results, check the label, add a minimum of sweetener, and then increase to taste.

• Liquid Sweetener Approximate* Equivalents

⅛ teaspoon liquid   = 1 teaspoon sugar
¼ teaspoon liquid   = 2 teaspoons sugar
½ teaspoon liquid   = 4 teaspoons sugar
¾ teaspoon liquid   = 6 teaspoons sugar
1 teaspoon liquid   = 8 teaspoons sugar
1½ teaspoons liquid = ⅓ cup sugar
1 Tablespoon liquid   = ½ cup sugar
2 Tablespoons liquid = 1 cup sugar

*Most sweeteners vary in sweetness according to the brand. For best results, check the label or add a minimum of sweetener and then increase to taste.

A Sprinkle of Words about Salt Substitutes

Because sodium can lead to water retention, which can be extremely frustrating when you're trying to lose weight, I've used "salt substitute" wherever I thought salt would add extra flavor in a recipe or a spice blend. However, some people just don't care for the taste of pure salt substitutes (potassium chloride) and prefer a blend of salt substitute and real salt. These products are usually labeled "Lite," and the label usually indicates that this is a salt substitute containing at least some of the real thing (sodium chloride).

If you have no problems with water retention as a result of sodium, you may even prefer to go ahead and use regular salt. Whether you use salt substitutes or the real McCoy, salt lightly to begin with and then slowly add more according to your taste. You can always increase the saltiness of foods, but it's difficult to perform a salt-ectomy once it's already been included.

All-American Spice & Herb Blends

1.

Butter Baby Blend

5 Tablespoons Butter Buds or Molly McButter Sprinkles

½ teaspoon salt substitute

1 Tablespoon dried parsley

SPICY IDEAS

Smooth As Butter Spread

Yield: 16 servings

8 ounces ricotta or farmer cheese
4 Tablespoons skim milk
2–3 Tablespoons **Butter Baby Blend** (to taste)

Blend all ingredients together in a mixing bowl until smooth and creamy. Refrigerate.

Per serving: 18 calories
.94 g fat
6 mg sodium
1.4 mg cholesterol

•

Butterball Veggies

Yield: 2 servings

⅓ cup coarsely chopped celery
8 ounces fresh or frozen peas
½ teaspoon thyme leaves
2 teaspoons **Butter Baby Blend**
Additional salt substitute to taste

In a tightly covered saucepan, cook the celery in ½ cup of water over medium heat for 5 minutes or just until tender. Add peas, cover the saucepan, and cook for 8 to 10 minutes more before draining well. Sprinkle peas with thyme and salt; toss with Butter Baby Blend until thoroughly moistened.

Per serving: 108 calories
.5 g fat
130 mg sodium
1.7 mg cholesterol

•

Skinny
Spices
Tip . . .

When you don't have the fresh herbs called for in a recipe but you do have the dried version, add a Tablespoon of chopped fresh parsley to each teaspoon of the dried herbs for an excellent substitute.

•

2.

Garlic Lover's Herb Blend

3 Tablespoons garlic granules or powder

1½ Tablespoons toasted sesame seeds

½ Tablespoon onion powder

1½ Tablespoons paprika

½ Tablespoon orange peel*

½ teaspoon ground red pepper*

*Dried form.

SPICY IDEAS

Vampire Chaser's Creamy Dressing
Yield: 1 cup (16 servings)

½ cup cottage cheese
½ cup low-fat buttermilk
½ lemon, peeled and seeded
4 chopped radishes
½ chopped green pepper
1 teaspoon salt substitute

. . . .

¼ teaspoon **Garlic Lover's Herb Blend**
Dash paprika

Place cottage cheese, buttermilk, and lemon in food processor or blender. Process or blend at high speed until smooth and velvety. Add all remaining ingredients, and pulse or blend at high speed until mixture is creamy and free of lumps.

> Per serving: 17 calories
> .4 g fat
> 35 mg sodium
> 1.3 mg cholesterol

●

Sublimely Garlicky Crab Cakes
Yield: 3 servings

6 ounces canned or frozen crabmeat
3 slices toasted bread
3 soft boiled eggs
Onion powder to taste
⅛ teaspoon **Garlic Lover's Herb Blend**
⅛ teaspoon dehydrated onion flakes
Dash pepper
Parsley flakes and paprika to taste
¼ cup low-sodium chicken bouillon

Crumble toast and mix with eggs and chicken bouillon. Then mix with all other ingredients and divide into three custard-type baking dishes. Bake at 350° for 20 minutes.

> Per serving: 219 calories
> 7 g fat
> 200 mg sodium
> 262 mg cholesterol

●

Skinny Spices Tip . . .

This suggestion is courtesy of Joe Cahn, founder of the New Orleans School of Cooking. To make a no-fat thickening agent, sprinkle flour on a shallow, non-stick cookie tin or baking pan and slow-bake in the oven at 325° for 1 hour. Use this "roux" to thicken soups or stews by combining with a *double* amount of cold water, and whisk it smooth or shake in a jar. Slowly whisk this mixture into a simmering soup or stew; it will thicken once it reaches 180°.

3.

Lemon Herb Blend

2 Tablespoons lemon peel*

1 Tablespoon basil*

½ Tablespoon ground thyme

½ Tablespoon ground oregano

½ Tablespoon paprika

½ Tablespoon toasted sesame seeds

2 teaspoons parsley flakes

1 teaspoon celery seed

1 teaspoon onion flakes

1 teaspoon garlic powder or granules

1 teaspoon cayenne pepper

*Dried form.

SPICY IDEAS
Wisconsin Cheese Log
Yield: 8 servings

4 ounces sharp Cheddar cheese, shredded
⅓ cup part-skim ricotta cheese
1 Tablespoon plus 1 teaspoon dry white
   wine
¼ teaspoon **Lemon Herb Blend**
Garlic powder to taste
Onion powder to taste
Salt substitute to taste
¼ cup minced fresh parsley

In blender or food processor, combine cheeses, Lemon Herb Blend, wine, garlic powder, onion powder, salt substitute and process until smooth. In the center of a sheet of plastic wrap, sprinkle 2 Tablespoons parsley, and then spoon the cheese mixture over the parsley in a line. Now sprinkle the remaining 2 Tablespoons of parsley over cheese, and enclose the cheese in wrap, forming a log about 6 inches long by 2 inches wide. Transfer to the freezer and let freeze for about 20 minutes; turn log over and freeze until firm, 10 to 25 minutes longer. To serve, remove plastic wrap and surround with Melba rounds.

Per serving: 80 calories
6 g fat
101 mg sodium
18 mg cholesterol

•

Decadent Veal Chops
Yield: 6 chops

6 loin veal chops
Salt substitute to taste
10 ounces low sodium beef bouillon or
   consomme
2 teaspoons **Lemon Herb Blend**

. . . .

1 Tablespoon Worcestershire sauce
½ chopped green pepper
½ cup chopped black olives
½ chopped onion
¼ chopped pimento

Sprinkle chops with salt substitute and Lemon Herb Blend. Brown on both sides under the broiler. Transfer chops to skillet and add all remaining ingredients. Now cover and simmer 40–45 minutes until veal is tender.

Per chop: 310 calories (approx.)
                9 g fat
                250 mg sodium
                207 mg cholesterol

●

Skinny Spices Tip . . .

For more flavor with less fat, use a teaspoon of sesame seed paste (tahini) to enliven homemade, low-fat, low-calorie salad dressings.

●

4.

Mild Garlic & Parsley Blend

6 Tablespoons parsley flakes

2 teaspoons garlic powder or granules

1 teaspoon onion flakes

1 teaspoon paprika

1 teaspoon finely ground black pepper

SPICY IDEAS

Deviled Fish Salad

Yield: 6 servings

½ cup plain yogurt
½ cup chili sauce
4 cups cooked white fish (halibut, sole, haddock, etc.)
½ teaspoon **Mild Garlic & Parsley Blend**
Lettuce
Pimento

Blend yogurt, chili sauce, and Mild Garlic & Parsley Blend together well. Toss gently with flaked fish. Serve on "cupped" lettuce leaves garnished with pimento.

Per serving: 230 calories
7 g fat
409 mg sodium
91 mg cholesterol

•

Garlic Toast

Yield: 2 servings

2 slices of 40-calorie white or wheat bread
1 Tablespoon diet margarine
½ teaspoon **Mild Garlic & Parsley Blend**

Brush bread with margarine. Sprinkle liberally with Mild Garlic & Parsley Blend. Slice bread in strips lengthwise. Bake in 350° oven for 10 minutes. Makes 8 "fingers" of garlic toast.

Per serving: 90 calories
3.7 g fat
243 mg sodium
0 mg cholesterol

•

Skinny
Spices
Tip . . .

For a tomato sauce with a Turkish accent, combine no-salt-added tomato sauce with bits of onion, garlic, hot pepper, cumin, cinnamon, black pepper, and parsley. Add olive oil to taste. Serve with grilled poultry or lamb.

•

5.

Pseudo Seasoned Salt Blend

1 Tablespoon mustard powder

1 Tablespoon garlic powder

2 teaspoons parsley

2 teaspoons dill weed*

2 teaspoons onion powder

2 teaspoons savory

2 teaspoons ground thyme

2 teaspoons paprika

2 teaspoons white pepper

1 teaspoon lemon peel*

*Dried form.

Pseudo Seasoned Salt Blend II

2 Tablespoons garlic powder

2 teaspoons ground basil

2 teaspoons ground marjoram

2 teaspoons ground thyme

2 teaspoons parsley flakes

2 teaspoons ground savory

2 teaspoons ground mace

2 teaspoons onion powder

2 teaspoons finely ground black pepper

2 teaspoons ground sage

1 teaspoon cayenne pepper

SPICY IDEAS
Chesapeake Bay Oyster Stew
Yield: 4 servings

1 pint shucked oysters
12 ounces clam juice
½ teaspoon of *either* **Pseudo Seasoned Salt Blend**
¼ teaspoon celery seed
Pepper to taste
2 cups skimmed milk
1 Tablespoon saltless diet margarine
1 teaspoon Worcestershire sauce
1 Tablespoon cornstarch
4 ounces canned water chestnuts, diced

Combine oysters and clam juice in the top of a double boiler and heat the mixture, but do not boil. Add Pseudo Seasoned Salt Blend, pepper and celery seed. Add milk, margarine, and Worcestershire sauce, but be careful not to allow the mixture to boil. Dissolve cornstarch in cold water and add to stew, cooking until thickened. Serve with water chestnuts as a low-calorie substitute for oyster crackers.

Per serving: 147 calories
4.6 g fat
466 mg sodium
67 mg cholesterol

●

Supremely Satisfying Vegetables
Yield: 8 servings

1 Tablespoon vegetable oil
1 cup diagonally sliced carrots
1 cup sliced cauliflower
½ cup sliced celery
½ cup sliced green pepper
¼ cup diced onion

¾ cup water
1 can bamboo shoots
1 cup fresh or canned water-pack pineap-
    ple chunks
2 Tablespoons low-sodium soy sauce
½ teaspoon of *either* **Pseudo Seasoned
    Salt Blend**
2 teaspoons cornstarch

Saute all vegetables in heated oil until coated and shiny
(a wok is ideal but a frying pan will do nicely). Add water;
cover and simmer for 10 minutes. Add bamboo shoots and
pineapple. Mix together all remaining ingredients and stir
into vegetables. Cook and stir until sauce begins to thicken,
about 2–3 minutes.

Per serving: 51 calories
         1.9 g fat
         278 mg sodium
         0 mg cholesterol

•

Skinny
Spices
Tip . . .

For a lean and lovely "cream" sauce base, combine 2
cups of part-skim ricotta cheese, ¼ cup cake flour, and 2
Tablespoons of fresh low-fat milk. Combine all ingredients
in food processor or blender. Use by the Tablespoon as a
low-calorie thickener for soups, sauces, stews, and other
dishes. Approximately 20 calories per Tablespoon.

•

6.

Classic Pepper Quartet Blend

2 Tablespoons coarsely ground black pepper

2 Tablespoons finely ground white pepper

2 Tablespoons finely ground green or pink pepper

1 Tablespoon finely ground cayenne pepper

SPICY IDEAS

Thick and Juicy Hamburgers

Yield: 6 burgers

1½ pounds lean ground beef
1½ teaspoons salt substitute
1½ teaspoons **Classic Pepper Quartet Blend**
1 Tablespoon freshly grated onion
1 teaspoon dried dill weed
¼ cup red wine

Mix beef together with all other ingredients and wine. Let the combination sit in the refrigerator for at least an hour to thoroughly combine flavors. Shape the meat into 6 patties, and broil or barbecue for 5 minutes on each side. Serve with tomato, onion, pickle, or your favorite hamburger garnish on a low-calorie whole-wheat bun.

Per burger: 316 calories
21 g fat
88 mg sodium
99 mg cholesterol

•

Chinese Restaurant
Sweet-and-Sour Chicken

Yield: 4 servings

1 fryer (2 pounds) cut up, with skin removed
½ cup wine vinegar
½ cup low-sodium soy sauce
2 cloves garlic, crushed
½ teaspoon **Classic Pepper Quartet Blend**
½ teaspoon salt substitute
1 teaspoon prepared mustard
¼ cup ketchup
2 Tablespoons honey
½ cup low-sodium chicken bouillon

Place chicken in 2-quart casserole and cover with sauce made from all remaining ingredients. Cover and bake at 325° for ½ hour until juicy and tender.

Per serving: 362 calories
8.3 g fat
500 mg sodium
133 mg cholesterol

•

Skinny
Spices
Tip . . .

For a tasty, economical alternative to ordinary hamburgers, try patties made from low-calorie ground veal. A food processor fitted with a steel blade quickly and easily does the job, or you can use a meat grinder. Start with veal cubes and add any of the following during processing: a clove of garlic, a few fresh basic leaves, a squirt of lemon, or a pinch of nutmeg.

7.

Vegetable Blend

1½ Tablespoons onion powder

1½ Tablespoons toasted sesame seeds

1 Tablespoon chives*

1 Tablespoon tarragon*

½ Tablespoon dry mustard

½ Tablespoon dill weed

1½ Tablespoon dried red bell pepper flakes

½ Tablespoon salt substitute

*Dried form.

. . . .

SPICY IDEAS
Garden Fresh Vegetable Spread
Yield: 1 cup (16 servings)

⅔ cup creamed low-fat cottage cheese
¼ cup minced green pepper
2 Tablespoons chopped pimento
Pepper to taste
1½–2 teaspoons **Vegetable Blend** to taste

Mix all ingredients well in blender or food processor, and use as a dip for veggies or as a spread on Melba toast, pitas, or low-calorie bread.

Per serving: 15 calories
.37 g fat
35 mg sodium
1.3 mg cholesterol

●

●

Squash Biscuits
Yield: 8 servings

1 12-ounce package frozen cooked squash
1 egg
1 teaspoon **Vegetable Blend**
1 Tablespoon flour
1 teaspoon baking powder

Defrost squash and drain well, patting completely dry with paper towel. Combine the squash with egg, flour, Vegetable Blend, and baking powder. Drop this mixture by heaping tablespoons onto a heated, non-stick frying pan (it also helps to coat it with non-stick spray) and heat until brown. Turn biscuits over to brown the other side.

Per serving: 35 calories
.67 g fat
50 mg sodium
27 mg cholesterol

●

 Skinny Spices Tip . . .

To liven up green beans, add any of the following skinny spices to melted diet margarine: marjoram, lemon juice, nutmeg, dill seed, dehydrated onion, curry, or basil.

●

8.

Fish Hater's Blend

1 Tablespoon savory

1 Tablespoon thyme

1 Tablespoon fennel

1 Tablespoon sage

1 Tablespoon marjoram

1 Tablespoon bay leaf

½ Tablespoon chives*

½ Tablespoon dehydrated onion

*Dried form.

* * * * * * * * * * * * * * * * * * *

Crabmeat Named Desire
Yield: 4 servings

1 10-ounce package frozen cauliflower
1 10-ounce package frozen spinach
1 teaspoon low-sodium chicken bouillon
  powder or granules
½ cup skim milk
½ teaspoon minced garlic
½ teaspoon **Fish Hater's Blend**
Salt substitute to taste
Pepper to taste
2 7-ounce cans crabmeat
1 Tablespoon grated Parmesan cheese
Paprika to taste

Cook cauliflower and spinach as directed on packages and drain well. Combine cauliflower, bouillon, skim milk, garlic, Fish Hater's Blend, salt, and pepper in blender and blend until smooth. Combine with spinach and crabmeat in 1-quart casserole. Sprinkle with cheese and paprika. Bake at 375° for 12–15 minutes or until golden.

Per serving: 140 calories
2 g fat
556 mg sodium
89 mg cholesterol

●

•

Country Ranch Dressing
Yield: 1 cup (16 servings)

1 cup buttermilk
1 packet low-sodium chicken bouillon
2 Tablespoons **Fish Hater's Blend**

Mix all ingredients together and chill.
Per serving: 12 calories
.17 g fat
80 mg sodium
.60 mg cholesterol

•

Skinny
Spices
Tip . . .

For an easy, light sauce to accompany a low-calorie fish dish, combine ½ cup salt-free diet margarine, 2 teaspoons grated lemon rind, and 3 Tablespoons lemon juice.

•

9.

Seafood Blend

2 Tablespoons toasted
sesame seeds

2 Tablespoons dill weed

2 Tablespoons paprika

1 Tablespoon garlic powder

SPICY IDEAS

Richer Than Rich
Chilled Shrimp Soup
Yield: 4 cups

½ lb. cooked and peeled shrimp
1 large cucumber, peeled and diced
1 large tomato, seeded and diced
1 quart buttermilk
Salt substitute to taste
Pepper to taste
Dash of Tabasco sauce
Dash of Worcestershire sauce
1 Tablespoon **Seafood Blend**

41

Mix together all ingredients in blender until smooth. Chill 24 hours and serve garnished with fresh dill or parsley.

Per cup: 177 calories
3 g fat
420 mg sodium
120 mg cholesterol

●

Velvety Tuna Casserole
Yield: 1 serving

2 ounces regular or hickory-smoked flaked tuna (water packed)
2 ounces farmer cheese
1 teaspoon canned or fresh mushrooms
1 teaspoon green pepper
1 teaspoon pimento
½ teaspoon **Seafood Blend**
Paprika

Season farmer cheese with Seafood Blend. Add tuna and remaining ingredients and place in baking dish. Sprinkle top with paprika. Bake at 350° for 20 to 30 minutes until crusty on top.

Per serving: 132 calories
.59 g fat
300 mg sodium
36 mg cholesterol

●

Skinny Spices Tip . . .

Experiment with spices that bring out the best in fish and seafood: basil, bay, chives, curry, dill, fennel, garlic, ginger, mustard, oregano, parsley, savory, and tarragon.

●

10.

Poultry Blend

2½ Tablespoons sage
2½ Tablespoons thyme
2 Tablespoons marjoram

SPICY IDEAS

Sexy Siren's Chicken

Yield: 4 servings

¼ cup low-sodium soy sauce
Juice of 1 lemon
1 teaspoon **Poultry Blend**
¼ teaspoon pepper
1 teaspoon ginger
2 lbs. chicken, cut up and skin removed
10 ounces thawed Chinese vegetables
4 ounces small cocktail onions

Combine all ingredients except vegetables and onions and pour over chicken. Let steep for 30 minutes or more. Brown chicken under broiler, basting it liberally with sauce. Transfer chicken to casserole, add Chinese vegetables, drained onions, and remaining marinade. Cover and bake in 350° oven for about 45 minutes or until tender.

. . . .

Per serving: 324 calories
7.2 g fat
700 mg sodium
159 mg cholesterol

●

Tangy Lime & Herb Turkey
Yield: 8 servings

3 pounds of turkey pieces

MARINADE:

1 cup tomato juice
½ cup reconstituted lime juice
⅛ teaspoon **Poultry Blend**
2 Tablespoons minced onion or dehydrated equivalent
2 teaspoons tarragon
1 teaspoon salt substitute
½ teaspoon hot sauce

Coat turkey in marinade and refrigerate for approximately 2 hours, turning occasionally. Bake in 400° oven
for 45 minutes, basting with sauce.

Per serving: 307 calories
8.6 g fat
233 mg sodium
130 mg cholesterol

●

Skinny Spices Tip . . .

For a spicy Latin American chicken marinade, combine equal parts orange and grapefruit juice plus ½ teaspoon grated grapefruit rind. Place chicken in a glass bowl, add juice and rind mixture, 2 mashed garlic cloves, and a generous pinch of cumin seeds or ground cumin. Cover and refrigerate for several hours before broiling or barbecuing.

11.

Meat Blend

2 Tablespoons rosemary

2 Tablespoons savory

1 Tablespoon thyme

1 Tablespoon marjoram

Meat Blend II

1 Tablespoon black pepper

1 Tablespoon garlic powder
or granules

1 Tablespoon onion powder

1 Tablespoon chili powder

½ Tablespoon lemon peel*

½ Tablespoon mustard seed

½ Tablespoon allspice

*Dried form.

½ Tablespoon coriander

½ Tablespoon marjoram

½ Tablespoon oregano

SPICY IDEAS
Shepherd's Pie
Yield: 6 wedges

8 ounces lean ground beef round
1 teaspoon of *either* **Meat Blend**
5 Tablespoons skim milk
1 cup biscuit mix
1 small onion, chopped
½ cup finely minced green bell pepper
2 tomatoes, peeled and diced
½ teaspoon oregano
½ teaspoon ground cumin
3 Tablespoons low-calorie mayonnaise
½ cup plain low-fat yogurt
½ cup shredded part-skim mozzarella
   cheese

Spread meat in a shallow layer on a broiler pan and brown under the broiler. Drain and discard all fat. Break meat into chunks and season with Meat Blend. Prepare non-stick pie pan by coating with cooking spray. Using two forks or a pastry blender, cut milk into biscuit mix until a soft dough forms. Spread dough in bottom and up the sides of pan. Put the browned beef in the bottom of the pie and sprinkle with onion, green pepper, tomatoes, oregano, and cumin. Blend mayonnaise with yogurt and spoon over top of pie; sprinkle with shredded mozzarella. Bake in preheated 375° oven for 30 minutes. Remove from oven and wait 5 to 10 minutes before slicing pie into six wedges.

Per wedge: 277 calories
12 g fat
443 mg sodium
47 mg cholesterol

●

Stick-To-Your-Ribs
Vegetarian Stew
Yield: 4 servings

9 ounces uncooked lentils
1 quart water
12 ounces pared potatoes, diced
1 cup diced onions
1 cup diced celery
1 cup diced carrots
¼ cup chopped fresh parsley
4 packets low-sodium beef broth and
   seasoning mix
2 teaspoons of *either* **Meat Blend**
1 bay leaf
⅛ teaspoon ground cumin

In 4-quart saucepan, combine lentils and water and bring to a rolling boil. Reduce heat to medium, cover pan, and let simmer on low heat for several hours until lentils are tender. Add remaining ingredients to lentils and stir to combine; cover and cook over low heat until potatoes are tender: 45 minutes to 1 hour. Remove bay leaf before serving.

Per serving: 297 calories
1.5 g fat
300 mg sodium
600 mg cholesterol

●

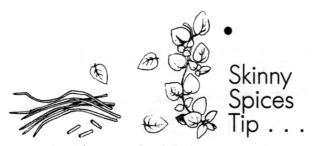

Skinny
Spices
Tip . . .

Avoid sugary barbecue sauces whenever possible. Instead, choose fruit juice or no-salt-added tomato juice to baste meats. You can add extra flavor with fresh herbs or liquid smoke seasoning.

12.

Cottage Cheese Blend

2 Tablespoons chives*

2 Tablespoons parsley flakes

1 Tablespoon celery seed

1 Tablespoon garlic powder

1 Tablespoon chervil

*Dried form.

SPICY IDEAS
Blue Ribbon
Cottage Cheese Dip
Yield: 8 servings

½ cup low-fat cottage cheese
½ teaspoon minced fresh onion
1 Tablespoon lemon or lime juice
½ teaspoon **Cottage Cheese Blend**
Dash of substitute salt
Dash of freshly ground pepper

Puree cottage cheese until smooth in food processor or blender. Combine all remaining ingredients and chill well.

Per serving: 16 calories
.15 g fat
57 mg sodium
.63 mg cholesterol

•

Egg-static Egg Salad
Yield: 1 serving

1 hard boiled egg, finely chopped
1 Tablespoon celery, chopped
½ teaspoon dehydrated onions to taste
⅛ teaspoon **Cottage Cheese Blend**
⅓ cup low-fat cottage cheese

Mix all ingredients well and serve on lettuce.
Per serving: 156 calories
8.3 g fat
349 mg sodium
222 mg cholesterol

•

Skinny
Spices
Tip . . .

An easy and tasty method for testing herb and spice combinations is to mix several herbs and spices into separate portions of light cream cheese or low-fat ricotta. After allowing the mixtures to sit at room temperature for one hour, spread on vegetables or Melba toast rounds, noting which flavors you like and which ones seem overpowering. Adjust seasonings until you discover exactly the right "formula," and write down all ingredients and measurements for future reference.

13.

Onion Pepper Blend

3 Tablespoons dried onion

2 Tablespoons coarsely ground black pepper

2 Tablespoons parsley flakes

SPICY IDEAS

Oniony Oven French Fries
Yield: 4 servings

2 medium potatoes
2 Tablespoons salad oil
1 teaspoon **Onion Pepper Blend**

Scrub potatoes but do not peel. Cut into wedges and place in a bowl of cold water for 15 to 20 minutes. Drain and pat dry with paper towels. Put wedges into a plastic bag and add salad oil. Shake to coat wedges lightly. Sprinkle Onion Pepper Blend over all surfaces of the "fries." On a non-stick cookie tin prepared with cooking spray, arrange potato wedges in a single layer. Bake in a preheated 500° oven for 12 to 15 minutes until potatoes are crisp and browned outside. Season to taste with salt substitute and paprika.

Per serving: 125 calories
6.9 g fat
300 mg sodium
0 mg cholesterol

●

Mushrooms Extraordinaire
Yield: 24 mushroom caps

24 fresh mushrooms (approx. 1 lb.)
½ cup chopped parsley
1 4-ounce can mushrooms, stems and
  pieces, finely chopped
2 Tablespoons minced fresh onion
2 Tablespoons powdered low-sodium
  chicken bouillon
¼ teaspoon **Onion Pepper Blend**
¼ cup water

Remove stems from fresh mushrooms and boil caps until tender. Chop reserved stems finely and add to remaining ingredients. Heat the mixture in a non-stick pan until tender. Stuff this mixture into mushroom caps, and spread them evenly on a cookie sheet. Bake at 375° for 20 minutes.

Per mushroom: 14 calories
2 g fat
.22 mg sodium
.12 mg cholesterol

●

Skinny Spices Tip . . .

Did you know that eating raw peppers in food can re-duce the chance of heart disease and aid circulation by in-creasing the production of fibrinolysin (a blood clot dissolver) in the blood? This keeps your blood flowing smoothly—and the increase in fibrinolysin can follow within 30 minutes of eating a pepper. That includes the mild varieties!

14.

Delicious Dill Blend

2 Tablespoons dill

2 Tablespoons onion flakes

1 Tablespoon garlic powder

1 Tablespoon toasted sesame seeds

½ Tablespoon lemon peel*

½ teaspoon dried cayenne pepper (optional)

*Dried form.

SPICY IDEAS
Luscious Yogurt Dip
Yield: 8 servings

8 ounces plain yogurt
1 raw cucumber unpeeled, finely chopped
1 medium clove of garlic, minced
½ teaspoon **Delicious Dill Blend**
Paprika

Pat cucumber dry in paper towel. Then combine with remaining ingredients and refrigerate for several hours to combine flavors. Sprinkle with paprika and use as a dip for fresh veggies or as a cool topping for a hot baked potato.

Per serving: 28 calories
.48 g fat
21 mg sodium
1.8 mg cholesterol

●

Dillightful Carrots
Yield: 4 servings

1 Tablespoon diet margarine
½ teaspoon **Delicious Dill Blend**
½ cup dry white wine
2 teaspoons minced onion
½ cup low-sodium chicken bouillon
2 teaspoons cornstarch
2 drops hot pepper sauce
3 cups hot, cooked sliced carrots

Melt margarine in saucepan; add Delicious Dill Blend, wine, and onion. Combine bouillon with cornstarch. Add to the contents of the pan, along with hot pepper sauce. Cook, stirring over moderate heat until sauce thickens. Add carrots, lower heat, and simmer 5 minutes.

Per serving: 96 calories
1.8 g fat
150 mg sodium
0 mg cholesterol

Skinny
Spices
Tip . . .

Use dill leaf rather than dill seed in cold, uncooked dishes since dill flavor is released more quickly from the leaf than from the seed.

Salad Spice Blends

15.

Tangy Tarragon & Herb Blend

1 Tablespoon tarragon

1 Tablespoon thyme

1 Tablespoon onion powder

1 Tablespoon dry mustard powder

1 Tablespoon coarsely ground black or red pepper

1 Tablespoon fennel

1 Tablespoon savory

SPICY IDEAS

Summer Pasta Salad
Yield: 4 servings

2 cups cooked spinach elbow macaroni,
   chilled
1 cup cooked cut green beans, chilled
1 medium tomato, chopped
1 ounce herb cheese (any type)
2 Tablespoons low-calorie mayonnaise
¼ cup plain low-fat yogurt
¼ teaspoon **Tangy Tarragon & Herb
   Blend**
Dash garlic powder
Dash freshly ground pepper

   Combine macaroni, green beans, tomato; set aside. In
small mixing bowl, using a fork, mash together cheese and
mayonnaise until cheese is completely blended; stir in yogurt, Tangy Tarragon & Herb Blend, garlic powder, and
pepper. Pour this dressing over macaroni mixture and toss
well to combine.

        Per serving: 155 calories
                 3.6 g fat
                 83 mg sodium
                 8.2 mg cholesterol

●

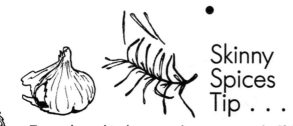

Skinny
Spices
Tip . . .

   To make a kinder, gentler vinegar, half fill a bottle with
crushed raspberries, strawberries, or other berries, then
cover the fruit with wine vinegar. Refrigerate for 1 to 2
weeks, then strain. Refrigerate again and use in salads or
for sauteing or stir-frying chicken or fish.

●

Herbed Superb Artichokes
Yield: 8 servings

2 10-ounce packages frozen artichoke
  hearts
½ cup water
1 Tablespoon olive oil
2 Tablespoons white wine
1 Tablespoon lemon juice
½ teaspoon salt substitute
4 peppercorns
1 bay leaf
1 clove garlic, crushed
½ teaspoon **Tangy Tarragon & Herb
Blend**

Combine all ingredients and simmer for 5 minutes until artichoke hearts are tender. Remove artichokes. Cook liquid uncovered for 10 minutes to reduce it. Strain liquid over artichokes. Chill for several hours or overnight. Serve cold.

Per serving: 55 calories
         2.1 g fat
         38 mg sodium
         0 mg cholesterol

Skinny Spices Tip . . .

Use thyme as a fragrant complement to meats, poultry, seafood, tomatoes, tomato-based sauces, salad dressings, marinades, and bastes.

16.

St. Tropez Salad Topping Blend

1½ Tablespoons chives*

1½ Tablespoons chervil

1½ Tablespoons parsley

1½ Tablespoons basil

1 Tablespoon celery seed

*Dried form.

St. Tropez Salad Topping Blend II

1 Tablespoon savory

1 Tablespoon garlic

1 Tablespoon oregano

1 Tablespoon basil

1 Tablespoon thyme

1 Tablespoon marjoram

½ Tablespoon finely ground black or cayenne pepper

½ Tablespoon paprika

SPICY IDEAS
String Bikini Beans
Yield: 6 servings

1 onion, chopped
1 clove garlic, minced
1 teaspoon oil
1 teaspoon of *either* **St. Tropez Salad Topping Blend**
1 tomato, peeled and diced
1 Tablespoon minced green pepper
1 Tablespoon minced celery
1 Tablespoon chopped parsley
1 Tablespoon dry white wine
Salt substitute
Pepper
1 pound string beans, cooked

Saute onion and garlic in oil until lightly browned. Add all remaining ingredients except beans. Simmer for 10 minutes. Pour sauce over cooked beans and mix well.

Per serving: 49 calories
1.1 g fat
6.7 mg sodium
0 mg cholesterol

●

Cold and Luscious
Riviera Soup
Yield: 2 servings

2 cups buttermilk
1 medium cucumber
1 packet low-sodium chicken bouillon
2 teaspoons dehydrated onion flakes
1 teaspoon dried dill weed
½ teaspoon of *either* **St. Tropez Salad Topping Blend**
1 teaspoon salt substitute
2 sprigs parsley

Peel and dice cold cucumber. Measure 2 cups buttermilk and pour into blender. Add all the other ingredients plus diced cucumbers. Blend for 3 minutes at medium speed. Taste and correct seasoning. Serve immediately in mugs or soup bowls. Garnish with parsley.

Per serving: 136 calories
2.7 g fat
385 mg sodium
9.3 mg cholesterol

Skinny
Spices
Tip . . .

Wondering what to do with chervil? Use it with fish, macaroni, potato and Caesar salads, or coleslaw. Or try adding it to low-calorie mayonnaise for use on sandwiches or in deviled eggs.

French
Spice
Blends

17.

Gallic Herbes Blend

3 Tablespoons chives*
2 Tablespoons tarragon
1 Tablespoon chervil
1 Tablespoon parsley flakes

*Dried form.

SPICY IDEAS

Parisian Bistro Steak
Yield: 6 servings

1½ pounds flank steak
¾ cup dry red wine
10 green onions, chopped
½ clove garlic, minced
1 teaspoon substitute salt
1 teaspoon rosemary
1 teaspoon pepper
¼ teaspoon **Gallic Herbes Blend**

Combine all ingredients and pour over flank steak. Marinate 1–2 hours, turning meat several times. Drain, reserving marinade. Broil steak 3–4 minutes on each side, basting with marinade, until medium rare. Cut diagonally, across grain of meat, into thin slices.

Per serving: 344 calories
21 g fat
73 mg sodium
95 mg cholesterol

●

Rosemary-Scented Spaghetti Sauce
Yield: 1 serving

6 ounces no-salt-added tomato juice
½ Tablespoon sweet red onion
¼ teaspoon garlic powder
¼ teaspoon **Gallic Herbes Blend**
½ teaspoon rosemary
Salt substitute to taste
Pepper to taste
Sugar substitute to taste
1 Tablespoon green peppers, finely chopped
1 Tablespoon mushrooms, finely chopped
1 teaspoon cornstarch

Simmer all ingredients together except mushrooms, green peppers, and cornstarch for 5 minutes. Add mushrooms and green peppers and simmer another 15 to 20 minutes. Dissolve cornstarch in a small amount of cold water and add to mixture. Cook until thickened and serve with pasta.

Per serving: 49 calories
.60 g fat
18 mg sodium
0 mg cholesterol

●

Skinny Spices Tip . . .

Instead of spaghetti for the recipe above, try this low-calorie alternative: drain a large can of bean sprouts. Place the sprouts in fresh water and cook ½ hour until soft. Drain thoroughly. Pour sauce over sprouts. Trust me, it tastes a lot better than it sounds.

18.

Provence Blend

2 Tablespoons rosemary

2 Tablespoons thyme

1 Tablespoon savory

1 Tablespoon fennel

1 Tablespoon basil

SPICY IDEAS

Totally Inebriated Chicken

Yield: 4 servings

1 fryer (2 lbs.), cut up and skin removed
1 cup canned tomatoes with liquid
½ cup white wine
1 clove garlic, minced
¾ teaspoon **Provence Blend**

Combine all ingredients and pour over chicken in shallow pan. Bake uncovered at 325° for 1½ hours. Baste frequently.

. . . .

Per serving: 313 calories
7.1 g fat
187 mg sodium
159 mg cholesterol

•

Ultimate Eggplant
Yield: 6 servings

1 Tablespoon olive oil
1 eggplant, peeled and diced
2 cloves garlic, minced
1 green pepper, diced
3 tomatoes, skinned and diced
½ pound fresh mushrooms, sliced
1 teaspoon salt substitute
2 teaspoons **Provence Blend**

Heat olive oil in skillet or wok and saute eggplant and garlic until lightly browned. Add remaining ingredients, including Provence Blend, and simmer, uncovered, 10 minutes until eggplant is tender.

Per serving: 72 calories
2.7 g fat
11 mg sodium
0 mg cholesterol

•

Skinny
Spices
Tip . . .

Rosemary can add a crowning touch to roast chicken, pork, shellfish, vegetables, and citrus fruit salads.

•

19.

Hearty Mustard Blend

2 Tablespoons dry mustard

2 Tablespoons mustard seed

2 Tablespoons parsley flakes

½ Tablespoon salt substitute

½ Tablespoon black pepper

SPICY IDEAS

Golden Temptation Chicken

Yield: 4 servings

1 fryer (2 pounds), quartered, skin removed
½ teaspoon curry powder
½ teaspoon **Hearty Mustard Blend**
1 Tablespoon honey
½ teaspoon grated orange rind
½ cup orange juice
½ teaspoon salt substitute
Dash pepper
2 oranges, peeled and sliced

73

Sprinkle chicken with curry powder and Hearty Mustard Blend, and rub mixture deeply into flesh to produce rich golden color. Place in shallow pan with skin side up. Combine honey, orange rind, juice, salt, and pepper. Pour over chicken. Cover with foil and bake at 325° for 2 hours, basting frequently. Garnish with orange slices.

Per serving: 336 calories
7.1 g fat
176 mg sodium
159 mg cholesterol

•

Salmon Dijonnaise
Yield: 4 servings

4 salmon steaks
¼ cup yogurt
2 teaspoons prepared Dijon mustard
½ teaspoon **Hearty Mustard Blend**
1 Tablespoon diet margarine
¼ cup apple cider

Spread salmon steaks with paste made from yogurt, prepared Dijon, and Hearty Mustard Blend. Melt margarine in skillet; add cider. Saute salmon in cider-margarine mixture for 10 minutes on each side.

Per serving: 194 calories
9.1 g fat
127 mg sodium
63 mg cholesterol

•

Skinny Spices Tip . . .

For a robust, creamy hollandaise sauce, combine 1 cup of buttermilk, 1 teaspoon lemon juice, sugar substitute to taste, ¼ teaspoon salt substitute, and ½ teaspoon **Hearty Mustard Blend**. Mix well and refrigerate before serving over fish or steamed vegetables.

Italian
Spice
Blends

20.

Checkered Tablecloth Italian Blend

1 Tablespoon garlic powder

1½ Tablespoons basil

1 Tablespoon thyme

1 Tablespoon oregano

1 Tablespoon rosemary

½ Tablespoon marjoram

½ Tablespoon sage

½ teaspoon cayenne pepper

SPICY IDEAS
Italian Seafood Salad
Yield: 6 servings

½ cup crabmeat
1 cup lobster meat
½ pound cooked shrimp
1 cup cooked white fish, flaked
2 tomatoes
1 cucumber, finely chopped
6 ripe olives, sliced
¼ cup plain low-fat yogurt
½ teaspoon celery seed
½ teaspoon salt substitute
½ teaspoon **Checkered Tablecloth Italian Blend**

Combine seafood with tomatoes, cucumber, and olives. Combine remaining ingredients for dressing and toss together. Serve in lettuce cups and garnish with pimento or parsley.

Per serving: 171 calories
3.6 g fat
318 mg sodium
128 mg cholesterol

●

Rat-A-Tatouille
Yield: 6 servings

1 medium eggplant, peeled and diced
1 Tablespoon hot olive oil (available in
  gourmet stores and by mail)
2 large onions, chopped
2 green peppers, diced
2 cloves garlic, crushed
2 zucchini, diced
1 16-ounce can tomatoes
Salt substitute to taste
Pepper to taste
2 Tablespoons chopped parsley
¼ teaspoon **Checkered Tablecloth Italian Blend**

Saute eggplant in olive oil; add and saute onions, peppers, and garlic. When vegetables begin to soften, add zucchini and tomatoes. Add all remaining ingredients, including Checkered Tablecloth Italian Blend. Cover and simmer 25 minutes; remove cover and simmer 10 minutes more to reduce liquid.

Per serving: 85 calories
2.6 g fat
463 mg sodium
0 mg cholesterol

Skinny
Spices
Tip . . .

For a fresh Italian tomato salad, combine 3 plum tomatoes cut into rings, 5 fresh scallions (tops included), **Checkered Tablecloth Italian Blend** to taste, and a dash of salt substitute and pepper.

21.

Mama Mia Pizza Blend

2 Tablespoons oregano

1 Tablespoon basil

½ Tablespoon onion flakes

½ Tablespoon garlic powder

½ Tablespoon thyme

½ Tablespoon fennel

½ Tablespoon paprika

½ Tablespoon coarsely ground black pepper

½ Tablespoon ginger

½ Tablespoon lemon peel*

*Dried form.

- - - - - - - - - - - - - - - - - - -

SPICY IDEAS
Pizza Craver's Pizza
Yield: 1 serving

⅓ cup no-salt-added tomato juice
⅛–¼ teaspoon dehydrated onion flakes (to taste)
Salt substitute to taste
⅛–¼ teaspoon **Mama Mia Pizza Blend** (to taste)
⅛–¼ teaspoon garlic powder (to taste)
1 teaspoon lemon juice
4 ounces canned salmon
1 slice low-calorie white bread
3 Tablespoons canned or fresh mushrooms

Simmer tomato juice with all seasonings and lemon juice. Break bread in very small pieces and put into bowl with salmon. Pour simmered mixture over bread and salmon and mix thoroughly. Press into 6-inch baking dish sprayed with non-stick vegetable spray. Arrange mushrooms on top. Bake in 350° oven for 15 minutes.

Per serving: 223 calories
7.4 g fat
157 mg sodium
68 mg cholesterol

●

Romantic Clam Chowder
Yield: 6 servings

2 cups no-salt-added tomato juice
Salt substitute to taste
1 12-ounce can clams with juice
1 teaspoon **Mama Mia Pizza Blend**
1–2 cloves garlic, finely chopped (to taste)
2 teaspoons "white" Worcestershire sauce

Simmer all ingredients together in pan or wok for 15 minutes. Serve hot with a garnish of fresh parsley or a twist of lemon rind.

> Per serving: 63 calories
> .68 g fat
> 176 mg sodium
> 20 mg cholesterol

•

Broccoli Around the Clock
Yield: 3 servings

1 lb. broccoli
1 cup water, salted with salt substitute
2 Tablespoons lemon juice
1 clove garlic, minced
¼ teaspoon **Mama Mia Pizza Blend**
¼ teaspoon salt substitute
Black pepper

Trim broccoli and simmer for 20 minutes in salted water until tender. Combine and heat remaining ingredients and pour over broccoli.

> Per serving: 53 calories
> .58 g fat
> 42 mg sodium
> 0 mg cholesterol

•

Skinny
Spices
Tip . . .

Use fennel with oily fish to minimize the fishy taste. Also try fennel in stir-fry oriental combinations or sprinkle on top of pork.

•

22.

California Chef's Pizza Blend

1 Tablespoon onion flakes

1 Tablespoon toasted sesame seeds

1 Tablespoon rosemary

1 Tablespoon basil

1 Tablespoon garlic

½ Tablespoon marjoram

½ Tablespoon oregano

½ Tablespoon ginger

½ Tablespoon mustard

* * * * * * * * * * * * * * * * * * * *

SPICY IDEAS

San Francisco Artichoke Hearts

Yield: 3 dozen

3 Tablespoons minced fresh onion
2 small cloves, garlic, crushed
2 cups low-sodium chicken bouillon
3 10-ounce packages frozen artichoke
   hearts
4 Tablespoons lemon juice
1 teaspoon salt substitute
¾ teaspoon **California Chef's Pizza Blend**

Cook onion and garlic in bouillon until tender. Add artichoke hearts, lemon juice, salt substitute, and California Chef's Pizza Blend. Simmer for 5 minutes until tender. Drain, chill, and serve.

Per artichoke heart: 18 calories
.19 g fat
95 mg sodium
0 mg cholesterol

●

Nouvelle Pasta Sauce
Yield: 1 serving

4 ounces tomato juice
3 packets low-sodium beef bouillon
1 Tablespoon dehydrated onion flakes
1 teaspoon **California Chef's Pizza Blend**
1 teaspoon parsley flakes
⅛ teaspoon garlic powder
Salt substitute to taste
Pepper to taste

Simmer all ingredients together for approximately 1 hour. Serve over pasta or spaghetti squash.
Per serving: 80 calories
1.7 g fat
400 mg sodium
1.8 mg cholesterol

Skinny
Spices
Tip . . .

Spices that work well in recipes that include low-calorie, low-fat cheeses include basil, caraway, celery seed, chervil, chili pepper, chives, coriander, cumin, curry, dill, garlic, horseradish, lemon peel, marjoram, mint, mustard, nutmeg, paprika, parsley, pepper, sage, tarragon, and thyme.

23.

Presto Pesto Blend

4 Tablespoons basil

2 Tablespoons minced garlic*

1 Tablespoon parsley flakes

*Dried form.

SPICY IDEAS
Presto Pesto Pasta
Yield: 1 serving

2 ounces cooked pasta (any type)
1 Tablespoon olive oil
2 teaspoons **Presto Pesto Blend**
Dash salt substitute to taste
Dash pepper to taste
⅛ teaspoon Parmesan cheese

Toss cooked pasta with olive oil. Add Presto Pesto Blend, salt, and pepper. Garnish with Parmesan cheese.

Per serving: 205 calories
14 g fat
4.7 mg sodium
.17 mg cholesterol

Uptown Bow-Ties

Yield: 3 servings

1 Tablespoon corn oil
1 large clove garlic, minced
½ cup finely chopped onion
½ cup finely minced red bell pepper
½ cup minced yellow or green bell pepper
½ cup low-sodium chicken bouillon
2 Tablespoons **Presto Pesto Blend**
1 teaspoon red pepper flakes (optional)
7 ounces bow-tie pasta, cooked and
  drained

In a large non-stick skillet, heat oil over moderately high heat. Add garlic, onion, and bell peppers; saute for 4 minutes. Stir in broth, Presto Pesto Blend and red pepper flakes if desired. Bring to a boil, stirring occasionally. Reduce heat and simmer for 4 minutes. Spoon over pasta and toss. Can be chilled and served over salad greens.

Per serving: 120 calories
5.4 g fat
250 mg sodium
0 mg cholesterol

Skinny
Spices
Tip . . .

Instead of using oil to help crush fresh basil for pesto sauce, try low-sodium chicken bouillon or low-fat ricotta cheese.

Mexican and Latin American Spice Blends

24.

Mild Chili Magic Blend

2 Tablespoons chili powder

1 Tablespoon cumin

1 Tablespoon oregano

1 Tablespoon garlic

1 Tablespoon salt substitute

SPICY IDEAS

Mexicali Rose Chip Dip

Yield: 16 servings

1 cup plain yogurt
2 teaspoons grated orange rind
¼ teaspoon **Mild Chili Magic Blend**
1 small dash granulated sugar substitute

Combine ingredients, refrigerate and use as a dip for carrot chips, fresh mushrooms, green pepper, and cauliflower florets.

Per serving: 14 calories
.21 g fat
10 mg sodium
.88 mg cholesterol

●

Fiesta Burgers
Yield: 8 burgers

2 pounds ground chuck
1 Tablespoon dehydrated minced onion
1½ teaspoons salt substitute
¾ teaspoon **Mild Chili Magic Blend**
¼ teaspoon pepper
⅛ teaspoon garlic powder

Combine all ingredients and mix lightly. Shape into 8 patties, each about ½-inch thick, and pan broil in hot skillet until desired doneness (bake if desired).

Per burger: 314 calories
17 g fat
80 mg sodium
120 mg cholesterol

●

Cowboy Chili
Yield: 3 servings

3 Tablespoons diet margarine
1 green pepper
2 ounces onions, cut thin
6 ounces ground beef
8 ounces tomato juice
1 Tablespoon **Mild Chili Magic Blend**
Salt substitute to taste
Pepper to taste
1 can bean sprouts, drained (optional)

Saute green pepper and onion in margarine, using non-stick pan that has also been coated with non-stick spray. Add crumbled ground beef and cook for 10 minutes, stirring constantly. Drain fat before adding tomato juice, Mild Chili Magic Blend, salt, and pepper. Cook until done. Add bean sprouts if extra volume is desired.

Per serving: 242 calories
16 g fat
541 mg sodium
49 mg cholesterol

Skinny
Spices
Tip . . .

Cumin seeds add South-of-the-Border flair to salads. Use about ⅛ teaspoon, along with a teaspoon of crumbled oregano. Serve with a cool, diet ranch dressing.

25.

Hot Cha Chili Blend

1½ Tablespoons cumin

1 Tablespoon onion powder

1 Tablespoon garlic powder

½ Tablespoon ground ginger

½ Tablespoon paprika

½ Tablespoon oregano

½ Tablespoon dry mustard

½ Tablespoon cayenne pepper

½ Tablespoon parsley flakes

SPICY IDEAS

South-of-the-Border Franks

Yield: 8 servings

1 large onion
2 cloves garlic, minced
1 cup lite ketchup
2 teaspoons **Hot Cha Chili Blend**
1 Tablespoon dry mustard
1 Tablespoon salt substitute
1 pound turkey frankfurters

Put all ingredients, except franks, into large, heavy saucepan or kettle with 2 cups water. Bring to a boil, cover, and simmer 15 minutes. Add franks and simmer 10 minutes longer. Serve franks topped with half of sauce. Serve remaining sauce tableside.

Per serving: 169 calories
11 g fat
936 mg sodium
49 mg cholesterol

•

•

Flame Kissed Roast Beef
Yield: 9 servings

3½ pounds sirloin of beef
2 teaspoons salt substitute
¾ teaspoon pepper
1 teaspoon **Hot Cha Chili Blend**
2 cloves garlic, minced
½ cup wine vinegar
½ cup water

Season meat with salt, pepper, Hot Cha Chili Blend and garlic. Marinate meat in fridge overnight in mixture of vinegar and water. Drain meat. Place meat on rack in roasting pan. Roast uncovered in a moderate oven at 350° until tender, allowing 20–22 minutes per pound for medium-well done.

Per serving: 365 calories
16 g fat
119 mg sodium
135 mg cholesterol

•

Skinny
Spices
Tip . . .

This make-your-own molé mixture adds a fast dash of Mexican flavor to diet foods:

1 Tablespoon ground cumin
1 Tablespoon dried oregano
1 Tablespoon ground cinnamon
1 Tablespoon plain, unsweetened cocoa powder
4 Tablespoons chili powder

•

Chinese
Spice
Blends

26.

Hunan Blend

2 Tablespoons toasted sesame seeds

1 Tablespoon ground black pepper

1 Tablespoon garlic

1 Tablespoon ground ginger

1 Tablespoon dried cilantro

½ Tablespoon mustard seed

½ teaspoon cayenne pepper

SPICY IDEAS

Plum Delicious Chinese Chicken

Yield: 4 servings

2 lbs. chicken breasts, split, with skin
6 ripe purple plums, pitted and thinly sliced
1 onion, halved and thinly sliced

. . . .

1 clove garlic, minced
3 Tablespoons water
2 Tablespoons lemon juice
2 Tablespoons light soy sauce
½ teaspoon liquid sugar substitute
1 teaspoon **Hunan Blend**

Brown chicken, skin side down, in an ungreased non-stick skillet or chicken fryer. Drain and discard chicken fat. Blot chicken with paper towel, remove skin, and return to the pan, skin side up. Add remaining ingredients *except low-calorie sweetener*. Cover and simmer, stirring occasionally, until chicken is tender—40–45 minutes. Uncover and continue simmering until sauce is thick. Add low-calorie sweetener only after cooking is complete and skillet has been removed from heat.

Per serving: 310 calories
7.3 g fat
346 sodium
159 mg cholesterol

•

Spicy Szechuan
All-Vegetable Stir-Fry
Yield: 4 servings

1 Tablespoon plus 1 teaspoon peanut oil
3 cups diagonally sliced asparagus (trim
   woody ends from 1 lb. asparagus)
1 cup diagonally sliced carrots
1 cup diagonally sliced celery
1 cup thinly sliced onions
1 medium red bell pepper, cut into strips
1 garlic clove, finely minced
¾ cup hot water
2 teaspoons dry sherry
2 teaspoons oyster sauce

1 teaspoon **Hunan Blend**
1 packet low-sodium beef bouillon
1 teaspoon cornstarch

Heat large wok or skillet; add oil and tilt wok or skillet to coat it evenly. Add vegetables, one at a time in order listed, stir-frying each for 1 minute. Add garlic and stir-fry for about 1 minute longer. In measuring cup or bowl, combine remaining ingredients, stirring to dissolve cornstarch; pour over vegetables, and cook until thick. Cover wok or skillet, reduce heat, and let cook until vegetables are tender-crisp or done to taste.

Per serving: 127 calories
5.1 g fat
200 mg sodium
.15 mg cholesterol

•

Skinny
Spices
Tip . . .

Here's a quick, tasty side dish that's a cool complement to spicy Chinese food: marinate cucumber slices and onion rings in rice vinegar. Add a dash of liquid sugar substitute. Sprinkle with toasted sesame seeds and serve.

•

Japanese Spice Blends

27.

Garlic & Ginger Blend

3 Tablespoons ground ginger

1½ Tablespoons garlic powder or granules

1 Tablespoon dried lemon peel

1 Tablespoon mustard powder

½ Tablespoon dashi (dried fish stock found in Japanese or oriental import stores or available by mail)

SPICY IDEAS
Beef Strips Hawaiian
Yield: 4 servings

1 lb. round steak, cut 2 inches thick
1½ teaspoons dry mustard
¾ teaspoon **Garlic & Ginger Blend**
1½ teaspoons black pepper
½ clove minced garlic to taste
6 Tablespoons low-sodium soy sauce
3 Tablespoons lemon juice
1 small eggplant, cubed
8 whole mushrooms

Chill steak well or partially freeze to make cutting into 1-inch strips easier. Place these strips in a shallow pan. Combine mustard, Garlic & Ginger Blend, pepper, and garlic with soy sauce and lemon juice. Pour over steak strips and marinate at least 4 hours. Parboil eggplant cubes 5 minutes, then drain. Thread steak strips on metal skewers, alternating with vegetables. Brush with marinade and broil 4 inches from heat, 6–7 minutes on each side.

Per serving: 261 calories
9.3 g fat
800 mg sodium
93 mg cholesterol

●

14 Carrots Gold
Yield: 4 servings

2 cups sliced carrots
Water, salted with salt substitute
2 Tablespoons diet margarine
½ teaspoon **Garlic & Ginger Blend**
Grated rind of ½ orange

Cook carrots in boiling, salted water 5–8 minutes and drain well. Melt diet margarine, and mix in Garlic & Ginger Blend and grated orange rind. Coat carrots thoroughly.

Per serving: 63 calories
2.9 g fat
120 mg sodium
0 mg cholesterol

Skinny
Spices
Tip . . .

Ground ginger makes diet oil-and-vinegar salad dressings sparkle. Use ⅛ teaspoon per cup of dressing.

28.

Japanese Horseradish Blend

5 Tablespoons wasabi (Japanese horseradish powder found in Japanese or oriental import stores or available by mail)

2 Tablespoons garlic powder

SPICY IDEAS

Dressing with a Kick

Yield: 16 servings

1 cup plain low-fat yogurt
¼ teaspoon **Japanese Horseradish Blend**
1 Tablespoon tarragon vinegar
1 Tablespoon chopped dill
1 Tablespoon chopped chives
1 Tablespoon sugar
¾ teaspoon salt substitute
¼ teaspoon paprika

Combine all ingredients. Cover and chill at least 4 hours.

Per serving: 18 calories
.23 g fat
10 mg sodium
.88 mg cholesterol

•

Wasabi Butter Sole
Yield: 2 servings

2 Tablespoons all-purpose flour
¼ teaspoon salt substitute
Dash pepper
Dash onion powder
Dash garlic powder
Dash paprika
2 sole fillets, 5 ounces each
1 Tablespoon plus 1 teaspoon diet
   margarine
½ teaspoon **Japanese Horseradish Blend**
1 Tablespoon chopped parsley

On sheet of wax paper, thoroughly combine flour and seasonings except for Japanese Horseradish Blend. Dredge fillets in mixture, coating evenly. In medium-size skillet, heat margarine until bubbly and hot; stir in Japanese Horseradish Blend. Add fish and cook over medium heat until browned on both sides. Sprinkle with parsley.

Per serving: 193 calories
5.3 g fat
204 mg sodium
68 mg cholesterol

•

Skinny
Spices
Tip . . .

Japanese horseradish (*wasabi*) also comes in paste form. Try blending a small amount (it's hot stuff!) with low-fat cottage cheese or ricotta cheese for a lively dip.

Indian
Spice
Blends

29.

Ceylon Curry Blend

3 Tablespoons curry powder

2 Tablespoons cardamon

1 Tablespoon cinnamon

1 Tablespoon ground black or cayenne pepper

SPICY IDEAS

Simply Divine Curry
Yield: 8 servings

2 chickens, cut in pieces, skin removed
1 cup plain low-fat yogurt
1 medium onion, finely chopped
2 cups water
1 green pepper, diced
½–1 Tablespoon **Ceylon Curry Blend** (to taste)
½ teaspoon salt substitute

Brown chicken pieces on all sides under broiler. Remove to a large pot or wok. Cover chicken with onions, yogurt, water, and Ceylon Curry Blend and simmer 15 minutes. Add green pepper and salt, and simmer 20–30 minutes or more until chicken is tender.

Per serving: 161 calories
3.9 g fat
108 mg sodium
81 mg cholesterol

•

Special "Sour Cream" Party Dip
Yield: 16 servings

⅔ cup low-fat cottage cheese
1 Tablespoon skim milk
1 Tablespoon lemon juice
¼–½ teaspoon **Ceylon Curry Blend** to taste

Blend all ingredients in electric blender, adding slightly more milk and lemon juice if necessary.

Per serving: 10 calories
.19 g fat
18 mg sodium
.66 mg cholesterol

•

Skinny
Spices
Tip . . .

For deliciously different deviled eggs, mash the yolks of hard boiled eggs with vinegar or lemon juice, powdered mustard, garlic, black pepper, a dash of curry powder, and low-calorie mayonnaise.

•

30.

Whisper of India Mild Curry Blend

1 Tablespoon ground ginger

1 Tablespoon garlic powder

1 Tablespoon turmeric

½ Tablespoon ground coriander

½ Tablespoon cumin

½ Tablespoon black pepper

½ Tablespoon mustard

½ Tablespoon fennel

½ Tablespoon cayenne pepper

½ Tablespoon allspice

SPICY IDEAS

Nirvana Veggies
Yield: 10 servings

1 head cauliflower, broken into florets
1 16-ounce bag frozen whole baby carrots
1 cup chopped green pepper
1 cup water
1 teaspoon salt substitute
3 Tablespoons vegetable oil
¼ teaspoon **Whisper of India Mild Curry Blend**

Combine all ingredients except oil and Whisper of India Mild Curry Blend; bring to a boil. Simmer, covered, until all vegetables are tender, about 15 minutes. Drain, coat with oil and Whisper of India Mild Curry Blend, and saute 3 minutes to combine flavors.

Per serving: 70 calories
4.2 g fat
31 mg sodium
0 mg cholesterol

●

Mughal Potato Curry
Yield: 6 servings

1 Tablespoon diet margarine
1 onion halved and sliced
1 green bell pepper, seeded and diced
3 potatoes, peeled and quartered
1 cup low-sodium chicken bouillon (or
   use 1 cup chicken broth skimmed of fat)
1½ teaspoons **Whisper of India Mild Curry Blend**
3 Tablespoons minced fresh parsley

In a saucepan, melt the margarine over moderate heat. Add onion and cook, stirring until translucent. Stir in pepper and potatoes. Add bouillon (or broth) and Whisper of India Mild Curry Blend. Cover and simmer until potatoes are nearly tender; about 20 minutes. Uncover and simmer until most of the liquid evaporates. Add minced parsley just before serving.

Per serving: 100 calories
1.2 g fat
150 mg sodium
0 mg cholesterol

Skinny
Spices
Tip . . .

For a quick, homemade curry powder, try this variation:

1½ Tablespoons ground coriander
1½ Tablespoons cumin
1 Tablespoon ground ginger
½ Tablespoon black pepper
½ Tablespoon red cayenne pepper

31.

Custom Curry Medium-Hot Blend

1 Tablespoon mustard powder

1 Tablespoon ground ginger

1 Tablespoon turmeric

1 Tablespoon cumin

1 Tablespoon allspice

1 Tablespoon cayenne pepper

½ Tablespoon fennel

. . . .

SPICY IDEAS
Scallops Taj Mahal
Yield: 20 skewers

1 pound bay scallops (or sea scallops cut in half)

2 cups cherry tomatoes

2 large green peppers cut into 1-inch pieces

⅓ cup lemon juice

2 Tablespoons unsweetened pineapple juice mixed with 1 packet of sugar substitute to sweeten

2 Tablespoons prepared mustard

1 Tablespoon oil

1½ teaspoons **Custom Curry Medium-Hot Blend**

Alternate scallops, tomatoes, and green peppers on 20 metal or wooden skewers. Place kabobs on well-oiled broiler pan. Combine remaining ingredients, and brush kabobs with this medium-hot sauce. Broil 4 inches from heat source for 3–5 minutes. Turn, brush with sauce, broil 3–5 minutes more, basting once.

> Per skewer: 50 calories
> 1.16 g fat
> 66 mg sodium
> 8.6 mg cholesterol

●

•

Madras Salmon

Yield: 1 serving

4 ounces canned salmon
1 Tablespoon non-fat dry milk in dry form
⅓ cup water
½ packet low-sodium chicken bouillon
¼ teaspoon **Custom Curry Medium-Hot Blend**
1 slice toast, using 40-calorie white bread

Mix salmon, milk, water, and Custom Curry Medium-Hot Blend in saucepan and heat. Add bouillon and stir in thoroughly. Pour over toast.

Per serving: 337 calories
7.7 g fat
300 mg sodium
69 mg cholesterol

•

Skinny
Spices
Tip . . .

For a homemade version of garam masala, an Indian spice blend required in many authentic recipes, use whole spices and grind the following ingredients into a powder:

2 Tablespoons black peppercorns
1½ Tablespoons cumin seeds
2 Tablespoon coriander seeds
1 Tablespoon cardamon seeds
1 inch cinnamon stick
5 cloves

117

Thai Spice Blends

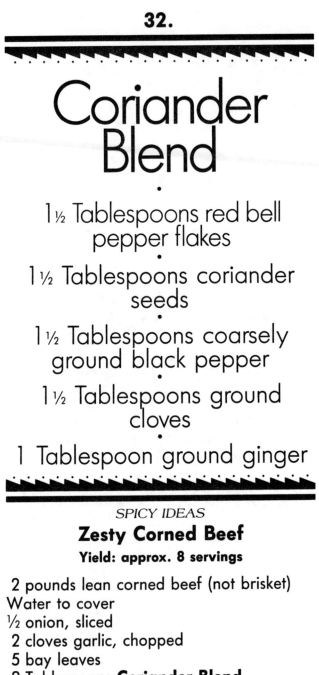

32.

Coriander Blend

1½ Tablespoons red bell pepper flakes

1½ Tablespoons coriander seeds

1½ Tablespoons coarsely ground black pepper

1½ Tablespoons ground cloves

1 Tablespoon ground ginger

SPICY IDEAS

Zesty Corned Beef

Yield: approx. 8 servings

2 pounds lean corned beef (not brisket)
Water to cover
½ onion, sliced
2 cloves garlic, chopped
5 bay leaves
2 Tablespoons **Coriander Blend**

. . . .

Place corned beef in a pot with water, cover, and simmer for 30 minutes. Discard water and replace with fresh water. Add onion, garlic, bay leaves, and Coriander Blend. Cover and simmer until meat is fork-tender—45–60 minutes, depending on size. Let cool to room temperature, then discard water and spices. Chill and slice thin.

> Per serving: 291 calories
> 17 g fat
> 1141 mg sodium
> 97.4 mg cholesterol

●

Golden Temple Chicken
Yield: 4 servings

4 pieces frying chicken thighs (or equivalent chicken parts), skinless
4 Tablespoons plain low-fat yogurt
2 Tablespoons lemon juice
2 Tablespoons vinegar
3 teaspoons **Coriander Blend**

Combine all ingredients (except chicken) for marinade. Cover chicken with mixture and refrigerate several hours. Arrange thighs in shallow broiler tray. Broil 6 inches from heat source for 15 minutes, turning and basting frequently with pan juices. Move 3 inches closer to heat source and broil. Turn frequently for 10–15 minutes longer until juices run clear.

> Per serving: 124 calories
> 5.6 g fat
> 51 mg sodium
> 50 mg cholesterol

●

Skinny
Spices
Tip . . .

For another Thai spice blend variation, combine chili peppers, dried cilantro, cumin, garlic powder, and onion powder.

33.

Bangkok Spice Blend

2½ Tablespoons toasted
sesame seeds

½ Tablespoon onion

½ Tablespoon chili powder

½ Tablespoon garlic

½ Tablespoon cayenne
pepper

½ Tablespoon coriander

½ Tablespoon nutmeg

½ Tablespoon cinnamon

½ Tablespoon dried lemon
peel

. . . .

SPICY IDEAS
Shrimp Curry Salad
Yield: 4 servings

2 cups cooked (1 lb. frozen) or 2 cans of
   shrimp sprinkled with lemon juice
½ cup diced apple
½ cup celery and leaves
¼ cup diced green pepper
½ teaspoon salt substitute
¼ teaspoon curry powder
¼ teaspoon **Bangkok Spice Blend**
¼ cup low-calorie mayonnaise
Lettuce leaves

Combine shrimp with apples, celery, and green pepper.
Add salt and spices to low-calorie mayonnaise. Combine
with salad mixture and toss lightly. Arrange in chilled lettuce cups.

> Per serving: 176 calories
>   4.3 g fat
>   344 mg sodium
>   225 mg cholesterol

•

Siam Stuffed Peppers
Yield: 2 servings

8 ounces water-packed tuna, well drained
   and flaked
½ cup celery, chopped
1 teaspoon dehydrated onion flakes, to
   taste
3 Tablespoons cider vinegar
Salt substitute to taste
Freshly ground black pepper
¼ teaspoon **Bangkok Spice Blend**
4 large green peppers

Blend tuna, chopped celery, dehydrated onion flakes, salt, pepper, Bangkok Spice Blend, and vinegar in a bowl. Chill for ½ hour. Remove tops from peppers and scoop out insides to make a cup. Sprinkle salt substitute on the insides of peppers. Spoon in tuna mixture and serve on bed of lettuce.

Per serving: 203 calories
.90 g fat
433 mg sodium
64 mg cholesterol

•

Skinny
Spices
Tip . . .

Try this flavorful sweet-and-spicy blend that's great on chicken or fish: cinnamon, ginger, pepper, and star anise.

•

Russian & Hungarian Spice Blends

34.

Old Country Caraway Blend

3 Tablespoons caraway

2 Tablespoons garlic powder

½ teaspoon black or cayenne pepper

SPICY IDEAS

Vegetable Hater's Brussels Sprouts
Yield: 4 servings

8 ounces canned tomatoes
1 green pepper, chopped
1 bay leaf
1 teaspoon **Old Country Caraway Blend**
½ teaspoon paprika
Salt substitute to taste
Pepper to taste
8 ounces Brussels sprouts, cooked and drained

Combine all ingredients except Brussels sprouts and simmer 8–10 minutes, until green pepper is tender. Cut cooked sprouts in half and combine with tomato mixture. Heat thoroughly.

Per serving: 43 calories
.50 g fat
99 mg sodium
0 mg cholesterol

●

Sweet 'n Sour Ambrosia
Yield: 4 servings

¼ cup low-fat plain yogurt
2 teaspoons white wine vinegar
½ teaspoon **Old Country Caraway Blend**
½ teaspoon salt substitute
½ teaspoon fresh lemon juice
2 cups thinly sliced celery
2 small Golden Delicious apples, cored and diced
¼ cup dark raisins
8 lettuce leaves

In medium bowl, combine yogurt, vinegar, Old Country Caraway Blend, salt, and lemon juice, mixing well. Add remaining ingredients except lettuce and blend thoroughly to combine. Chill for 30 minutes before serving.

Per serving: 100 calories
.67 g fat
67 mg sodium
.88 mg cholesterol

●

129

Skinny
Spices
Tip . . .

For hearty coleslaw without added fat, add $\frac{1}{4}$ teaspoon of anise seeds. This is an especially nice addition when the slaw contains bits of pineapple or chopped apple.

35.

Paprika Blend

3½ Tablespoons paprika
3½ Tablespoons dill

SPICY IDEAS
Delectable Herb Dressing
Yield: 16 servings

2 teaspoons prepared horseradish
1 Tablespoon tarragon vinegar
¼ cup lemon juice
¾ cup water
Sugar substitute to equal 1 Tablespoon of
    sugar
1 teaspoon salt substitute
1 teaspoon **Paprika Blend**
2 cups non-fat dry milk powder

Combine all ingredients in electric blender. Blend for 30 seconds or until smooth. Chill for about 2 hours.

Per serving: 37 calories
.08 g fat
47 mg sodium
1.5 mg cholesterol

●

Incredible Edible Spread
Yield: 1 serving

4 ounces water-packed tuna, drained
1 teaspoon dehydrated onion flakes
2 teaspoons **Paprika Blend**
2 teaspoons non-fat dry milk
1 Tablespoon water
Celery and green pepper slices

Place all ingredients except celery and green pepper slices in electric blender or food processor. Blend or process at low speed for 30 seconds. Garnish with celery and green pepper slices.

Per serving: 179 calories
.69 g fat
446 mg sodium
64 mg cholesterol

●

 Skinny
Spices
Tip . . .

There are two types of paprika: the more pungent Hungarian variety is a must for goulash and chicken paprikash. The milder Spanish variety, the most common type found in the United States, is used mainly as a garnish.

●

Greek and Mid-Eastern Spice Blends

36.

Garlic & Lemon Twist Blend

2 Tablespoons garlic powder

2 Tablespoons dried lemon peel

1 Tablespoon coarsely ground black pepper

1 Tablespoon finely ground green pepper

1 Tablespoon finely ground white or pink pepper

* *

SPICY IDEAS

Vestal Virgins' Dip
Yield: 16 servings

1 clove fresh garlic, finely minced
3 walnut meats, grated
1 teaspoon olive oil
1 cup plain, low-fat yogurt
1 small, unpeeled cucumber, diced
¼ teaspoon **Garlic & Lemon Twist Blend**

Combine garlic and nuts with oil in food processor, and puree into a smooth paste. Stir into yogurt, add cucumber, season with Garlic & Lemon Twist Blend to taste. Refrigerate several hours to combine flavors. Great as a dip for cucumbers, carrots, zucchini, and green peppers.

Per serving: 31 calories
1.6 g fat
11 mg sodium
.88 mg cholesterol

•

Belly Dancer's
Cauliflower

Yield: 4 servings

1 whole cauliflower
½ cup chicken bouillon from low-sodium
   granules
1 Tablespoon low-sodium soy sauce
1 teaspoon **Garlic & Lemon Twist Blend**

Simmer cauliflower in chicken bouillon until tender about 20 minutes. Drain and sprinkle with soy sauce and Garlic & Lemon Twist Blend.

Per serving: 37 calories
.35 g fat
200 mg sodium
0 mg cholesterol

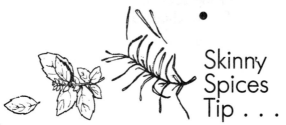

Skinny
Spices
Tip . . .

For a quick summer herb blend, combine basil, marjoram, rosemary, and thyme.

37.

Open Sesame Blend

4 Tablespoons toasted sesame seeds

1 Tablespoon onion flakes

½ Tablespoon paprika

½ Tablespoon garlic powder

½ Tablespoon dried lemon peel

½ Tablespoon cayenne pepper

SPICY IDEAS
Cute As Can Be Cukes
Yield: 4 servings

2 medium cucumbers
2 teaspoons salt substitute
½ cup white vinegar
1½ teaspoons liquid sugar substitute
2 teaspoons minced fresh ginger root
2 teaspoons **Open Sesame Blend**

Wash cucumbers and pare lengthwise into ¼-inch strips, leaving every other strip of green skin on. Cut in halves, lengthwise, remove seeds, and slice thinly. Put in bowl and add salt substitute. Mix well and let stand 1 hour. Place cucumbers in cheesecloth and squeeze out any excess moisture. Mix remaining ingredients and bring to a boil. Pour over cucumbers and chill several hours.

Per serving: 38 calories
.95 g fat
3.6 mg sodium
0 mg cholesterol

●

•

Curried Sesame Sauce
Yield: 8 servings

½ cup buttermilk
1 Tablespoon bottled white horseradish
2 Tablespoons low-sodium ketchup
1 teaspoon lemon juice
1 teaspoon curry powder
2 teaspoons **Open Sesame Blend**
½ teaspoon finely ground pepper

Combine all ingredients, mix thoroughly, and chill.
Per serving: 22 calories
.56 g fat
64 mg sodium
.56 mg cholesterol

•

Skinny
Spices
Tip . . .

Enhance the nutty flavor of sesame seeds by toasting or browning before adding them to salads for a nutritious topping. Toast by spreading seeds on a shallow cooking tin in a hot oven for a few minutes. Or shake them in a non-stick skillet over high heat. Let cool and store in covered jar.

•

38.

Moroccan Mint Blend

2 Tablespoons dried mint leaves

2 Tablespoons garlic granules or powder

2 Tablespoons toasted sesame seeds

½ Tablespoon dried lemon peel

½ Tablespoon onion flakes

SPICY IDEAS
Lamb Kabobs
Yield: 6 servings

1 teaspoon **Moroccan Mint Blend**
½ cup dry red wine
¼ cup red wine vinegar
1 clove garlic, minced
1 teaspoon salt substitute
¼ teaspoon pepper
1½ pounds boned lamb, cut into 1-inch cubes

Combine Moroccan Mint Blend, wine, vinegar, garlic, salt, and pepper. Pour over lamb and marinate at least 1 hour. Drain, reserving marinade. Place lamb on skewers and broil 20 minutes, coating frequently with marinade.

Per serving: 280 calories
14 g fat
93 mg sodium
100 mg cholesterol

•

Marakesh Delight Cream Soup

Yield: 4 cups

1 cup plain low-fat yogurt
¼ cup all-purpose flour
4 cups low-sodium chicken broth
½ teaspoon **Moroccan Mint Blend**

Stir yogurt and flour together in a saucepan. Gradually add chicken broth, bring to a boil, and stir over medium heat for 5 minutes. Add Moroccan Mint Blend and heat for 1 minute more. Serve hot or cold, and garnish with fresh parsley or a mint leaf.

Per cup: 88 calories
2 g fat
250 mg sodium
3.5 mg cholesterol

•

Skinny Spices Tip . . .

Do as the French do, and toss some melted diet margarine and mint into cooked vegetables just before serving.

•

39.

Savory Tarragon Blend

2 Tablespoons tarragon

1 Tablespoon onion flakes

1 Tablespoon mustard powder

1 Tablespoon black pepper

1 Tablespoon fennel

1 Tablespoon savory

SPICY IDEAS
Grecian Goddess Zucchini
Yield: 10 servings

1 Tablespoon chopped parsley
1 teaspoon **Savory Tarragon Blend**
Pinch thyme
½ teaspoon salt substitute
Dash pepper
2 drops hot sauce
1 bay leaf
2 Tablespoons lemon juice
2 cloves garlic, minced fine
1 cup red wine
1 pound zucchini, sliced ¼-inch thick

Combine all ingredients except zucchini in saucepan. Bring to a boil, then add zucchini and simmer 5–10 minutes or until tender. Cool and refrigerate in remaining liquid. Drain and serve.

Per serving: 30 calories
.08 g fat
2.6 mg sodium
0 mg cholesterol

●

Mykonos Mushroom Soup
Yield: 3 cups

1 medium onion
1 cup low-sodium chicken bouillon
2 cups tomato juice
1 lb. fresh mushrooms, sliced
1 teaspoon **Savory Tarragon Blend**

Saute onion in bouillon in a 3-quart, non-stick saucepan. Add tomato juice and Savory Tarragon Blend and simmer for 30 minutes, stirring occasionally. Add mushrooms and simmer for 15 minutes more.

Per cup:	83 calories
	1.1 g fat
	250 mg sodium
	0 mg cholesterol

Skinny
Spices
Tip . . .

Savory is a great complement to bean dishes. It's also good with game, roast turkey, and low-calorie meat loaf.

Hot Spice Blends

40.

Cajun Blend

1 Tablespoon chili powder

1 Tablespoon paprika

1 Tablespoon onion flakes

1 Tablespoon garlic powder

1 Tablespoon allspice

1 Tablespoon cayenne pepper

1 Tablespoon thyme

· · · · · · · · · · · · · · · · · · ·

SPICY IDEAS

Voodoo Queen Vegetables

Yield: 4 servings

2 medium zucchini
10 ounces canned tomatoes
1 small green onion or dehydrated
  equivalent
½ stalk celery
¼ green pepper
Sugar substitute to taste
Salt substitute to taste
Pepper to taste
½ teaspoon **Cajun Blend**

Wash zucchini, cut ends off, and cut into 1-inch pieces.
Put into saucepan with all remaining ingredients. Cook
over low heat, uncovered, until tender.

Per serving: 35 calories
.32 g fat
122 mg sodium;
0 mg cholesterol

●

French Market Tomato Soup

Yield: 2 servings

12 ounces no-salt-added tomato juice
1 small clove garlic, mashed
1 Tablespoon red onion
2 Tablespoons parsley, chopped
1 Tablespoon wine vinegar
½ package low-sodium beef bouillon
¼ teaspoon **Cajun Blend**
Pepper to taste

Put garlic and onion into food processor and liquefy. Add all other ingredients and process for 2–3 minutes. Serve hot or cold with cucumber slices.

Per serving: 39 calories
.30 g fat
273 mg sodium
.15 mg cholesterol

Skinny
Spices
Tip . . .

Use allspice with soups, seafood, poultry, and fruit salads. Its scent will make you think of a blend of cinnamon, cloves, and nutmeg.

41.

5-Alarm Hot Stuff

1 Tablespoon granulated garlic

1 Tablespoon onion flakes

1 Tablespoon red pepper flakes

½ Tablespoon ground ginger

½ Tablespoon thyme

½ Tablespoon mustard powder

½ Tablespoon ground cloves

½ Tablespoon coarsely
ground black pepper

½ Tablespoon paprika

½ Tablespoon cumin

1 teaspoon bay leaf

1 teaspoon parsley flakes

*   *   *   *   *   *   *   *   *   *   *   *   *   *   *

SPICY IDEAS
Vegetables from Hell
Yield: 6 servings

½ cup dried shitake mushrooms
1 cup celery, sliced
1 7-ounce package frozen pea pods
1 teaspoon low-sodium soy sauce
½ teaspoon **5-Alarm Hot Stuff**

Pour warm water over mushrooms to cover, and let sit for 20 minutes to soften. Drain and slice. Cook celery in salted water for 5 minutes. Cook pea pods as directed on package. Toss all vegetables together with soy sauce and 5-Alarm Hot Stuff.

Per serving: 82 calories
.34 g fat
40 mg sodium
0 mg cholesterol

●

Hotsy Totsy
Mustard Dressing
Yield: 8 servings

1 Tablespoon prepared mustard
2 Tablespoons lemon juice
⅛ teaspoon 5-Alarm Hot Stuff
⅔ cup non-fat skim milk powder
⅔ cup water
½ teaspoon salt substitute
Dash freshly ground pepper
½ teaspoon sugar substitute

Blend all ingredients together and store in fridge.

Per serving: 28 calories
.14 g fat
55 mg sodium
.99 mg cholesterol

•

Skinny
Spices
Tip . . .

For a quick hot-and-spicy herb blend, combine basil,
bay, oregano, parsley, and red pepper flakes.

•

42.

Southwestern Fire

1 Tablespoon granulated
onion

1 Tablespoon paprika

1 Tablespoon chili powder

1 Tablespoon cumin

½ Tablespoon garlic

½ Tablespoon cayenne
pepper

½ Tablespoon ground
coriander

½ Tablespoon oregano

½ Tablespoon dried lemon
peel

. . . .

SPICY IDEAS
Santa Fe Dressing
Yield: 8 servings

8 ounces buttermilk
2 teaspoons horseradish
¼ teaspoon **Southwestern Fire**
¼ teaspoon salt substitute
1 teaspoon minced onion

Combine all ingredients; blend well and refrigerate.
Per serving: 17 calories
.25 g fat
31 mg sodium
1 mg cholesterol

●

Liquid Dynamite
Crab Bisque
Yield: 2 servings

2 cups skim milk
1 stalk celery, cut up
1 small onion or equivalent dehydrated
1 bay leaf
½ teaspoon salt substitute
½ teaspoon **Southwestern Fire**
8 ounces frozen crab meat
Minced parsley

Heat milk with celery, onions, and bay leaf. Strain after simmering for 15 minutes. Stir together seasoned milk, salt, and Southwestern Fire. Add frozen crab meat. Simmer over low heat until crab thaws and separates, stirring frequently. Garnish with minced parsley.

· · · · · · · · · · · · · · · · · · ·

Per serving: 218 calories
2.5 g fat
455 mg sodium
117 mg cholesterol

●

Skinny
Spices
Tip . . .

Cumin adds an especially delightful accent to yogurt-based dishes and dips.

●

43.

Zippy Pepper Blend

1 Tablespoon black pepper

1 Tablespoon thyme

1 Tablespoon marjoram

1 Tablespoon tarragon

1 Tablespoon basil

1 Tablespoon dried chives

1 Tablespoon hot red pepper flakes

SPICY IDEAS

Very Special Creamy Pepper Dressing

Yield: 8 servings

1 Tablespoon no-salt-added tomato juice
½ teaspoon oregano
½ teaspoon marjoram
½ teaspoon paprika
½ teaspoon **Zippy Pepper Blend**

¼ teaspoon dry mustard
½ clove garlic, pureed
1 cup buttermilk

Mix all seasonings and tomato juice. Add buttermilk and mix well.

Per serving: 14 calories
.30 g fat
33 mg sodium
1.1 mg cholesterol

●

Sinful Creamed Mushrooms

Yield: 1 serving

1 slice low-calorie bread
2 ounces low-fat cottage cheese
2 ounces canned mushrooms
1 packet low-sodium chicken bouillon
¼ teaspoon **Zippy Pepper Blend**

Toast one side of bread and place toasted side down on aluminum foil. Combine all other ingredients. Heap on bread. Broil until cottage cheese is melted and slightly brown.

Per serving: 256 calories
4 g fat
300 mg sodium
9 mg cholesterol

●

 Skinny
Spices
Tip . . .

Try seasoning your next low-calorie Mexican dish with a combination of chili pepper, fresh cilantro, oregano, garlic, and lime juice.

●

44.

Jamaican Scorcher Blend

1 Tablespoon ground ginger

1 Tablespoon mustard seed

1 Tablespoon granulated onion

½ Tablespoon allspice

½ Tablespoon granulated garlic

½ Tablespoon paprika

½ Tablespoon thyme

½ Tablespoon dried lemon peel

½ Tablespoon coarsely ground black pepper

½ Tablespoon hot red pepper flakes

½ Tablespoon ground cloves

. . . .

SPICY IDEAS
Kingston Killer Dressing
Yield: 12 servings

1 cup plain low-fat yogurt
½ cup chili sauce
¼–½ teaspoon **Jamaican Scorcher Blend**
(depending on your pain threshold)

Blend thoroughly and chill. Great with exotic veggies such as jicama or steamed baby zucchini.

Per serving: 29 calories
.32 g fat
165 mg sodium
1.2 mg cholesterol

•

Ochos Rios Haddock
Yield: 4 servings

1 pound haddock fillet
1 lemon, seeded and cut up with peel
½ clove garlic
1 stalk celery, diced
1 Tablespoon Worcestershire sauce
1 teaspoon oregano
1 teaspoon parsley flakes
1 teaspoon horseradish
½ teaspoon **Jamaican Scorcher Blend**

Put all ingredients except fish into blender and chop well for about 15 seconds. Cut fish into individual servings and wrap in foil. Before closing foil, spoon chopped mixture evenly over fish. Close tightly and bake in preheated oven at 325° for 45 minutes.

Per serving: 106 calories
.93 g fat
256 mg sodium
65 mg cholesterol

•

Skinny
Spices
Tip . . .

To create interesting low-calorie mustard blends, combine mustard powder with wine, beer, or even skimmed milk. Add extra flavor with marjoram, tarragon, chervil, or chives.

•

Sweet Spice Blends

45.

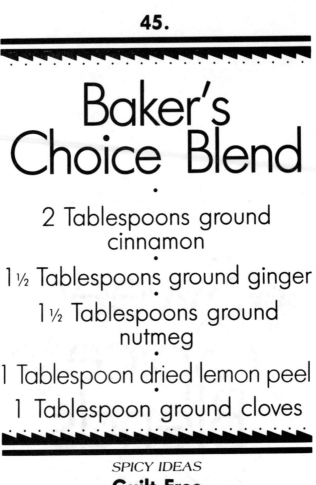

Baker's Choice Blend

2 Tablespoons ground cinnamon

1½ Tablespoons ground ginger

1½ Tablespoons ground nutmeg

1 Tablespoon dried lemon peel

1 Tablespoon ground cloves

SPICY IDEAS

Guilt-Free Apple Pie

Yield: 4 servings

4 apples, peeled, cored, and sliced
1 12-ounce can low-calorie lemon-lime soda
1 package unflavored gelatin
Sweetener (equal to 4 teaspoons sugar)
⅓ cup dry non-fat milk
½ teaspoon **Baker's Choice Blend**

. . . .

Dissolve sugar substitute in gelatin, and ½ of the dry milk in lemon-lime soda. Arrange apples in 8-inch cake pan. Spoon liquid over it carefully. Sprinkle remainder of dry milk over top and dust with Baker's Choice Blend. Bake in 350° oven for 1 hour. Cool and refrigerate.

> Per serving: 157 calories
> .80 g fat
> 48 mg sodium
> .99 mg cholesterol

●

Pineapple Frozen Solids
Yield: 2 servings

16 ounces buttermilk
 4 ounces unsweetened crushed pineapple
 1 Tablespoon sugar substitute (or more to taste)
⅛ teaspoon **Baker's Choice Blend**

Mix all ingredients together and spill into an ice cube tray. Put in coldest part of your freezer for 1½ hours. Pop out and enjoy!

> Per serving: 131 calories
> 2 g fat
> 239 mg sodium
> 8.3 mg cholesterol

●

Skinny Spices Tip . . .

Spices can add a new dimension to fruit desserts and make them seem extra-special:

apples with cinnamon
peaches with ginger
pears with clove
oranges with cinnamon or clove
sliced grapes with allspice or nutmeg

46.

Sweet Treat Blend

2½ Tablespoons ground nutmeg

2½ Tablespoons ground vanilla bean

2 Tablespoons powdered or granular sugar substitute

SPICY IDEAS

Knockout Sweet Roll

Yield: 4 servings

6 ounces farmer or ricotta cheese
1 large egg
1 capful vanilla
Sugar substitute equal to 6 teaspoons of sugar (or to taste)
⅛ teaspoon **Sweet Treat Blend**
3 Tablespoons crushed pineapple or fresh peaches
2 pieces low-calorie bread, toasted and divided into quarters

Mix first five ingredients with a fork, and spread half on each slice of bread. Spread crushed pineapple or peach bits on top, and broil until lightly browned.

Per serving: 149 calories
1.9 g fat
190 mg sodium
56 mg cholesterol

•

Tropical Nights
Bread Pudding
Yield: 2 servings

1 cup skim milk
Liquid egg substitute to equal 1 egg
Liquid sugar substitute to equal 6
     teaspoons sugar
½ teaspoon coconut extract
½ teaspoon pineapple extract
½ teaspoon vanilla extract
1½ slices 40-calorie white or wheat bread,
     cubed
Sweet Treat Blend to taste

Combine all ingredients except bread and Sweet Treat Blend in the blender or food processor and process until frothy. Pour mixture into small baking dish, and press bread cubes into mixture to soak up liquid. Sprinkle with Sweet Treat Blend to taste. Place baking dish in a pan with ½ inch of very hot tap water. Bake at 350° for 50 minutes, until knife comes out clean. Eat hot or cold.

Per serving: 95 calories
1.57 g fat
171 mg sodium
2.3 mg cholesterol

•

Skinny
Spices
Tip . . .

Indulge in Skinny Cinnamon Toast: toast low-calorie bread in oven or toaster, sprinkle powdered sugar substitute plus **Sweet Treat Blend** on bread, and then toast again. A few drops of skim milk brushed over the bread before sprinkling will help the sweetener adhere to the surface.

47.

Choc-o-holic Blend

3 Tablespoons unsweetened cocoa powder

3 Tablespoons powdered or granular sugar substitute

1 Tablespoon cinnamon

SPICY IDEAS
Thick and Creamy Chocolate Lover's Shake
Yield: 1 serving

1 cup skim milk
1 teaspoon chocolate extract
¼ teaspoon **Choc-o-holic Blend**
½ teaspoon instant decaffeinated coffee
4–5 ice cubes

Place all ingredients in blender for about 30 seconds. Add additional ice cube if extra thickness is desired.

Per serving: 97 calories
.44 g fat
126 mg sodium
4 mg cholesterol

•

Chocolate Rum Custard
Yield: 1 serving

4 ounces undiluted evaporated skim milk
½ teaspoon rum extract
½ teaspoon vanilla extract
1 teaspoon **Choc-o-holic Blend**
¾ teaspoon liquid sugar substitute
8 large ice cubes

Place all ingredients except ice into blender. Start blender and add ice one cube at a time. When mixture reaches the consistency of frozen custard, spoon into chilled glasses.

Per serving: 99 calories
.23 g fat
130 mg sodium
4.5 mg cholesterol

•

Skinny
Spices
Tip . . .

Add a dash of cinnamon to your next batch of spaghetti sauce, and liven up an old Italian favorite.

•

48.

Indian Dessert Blend

2 Tablespoons cardamon*

2 Tablespoons allspice

2 Tablespoons cinnamon

1 Tablespoon powdered or granular sugar substitute

*Ground form.

SPICY IDEAS

Coconut Apple Crunch Cookies

Yield: 20 cookies

¾ cup grated apple
6 Tablespoons brown sugar substitute
½ teaspoon coconut extract or vanilla extract
½ teaspoon **Indian Dessert Blend**
1⅓ cup non-fat dry milk (powder form)

Mix all ingredients in mixing bowl. Drop by teaspoonfuls onto non-stick cookie sheet or cookie sheet sprayed with non-stick spray. Bake in 350° oven for approximately 15 minutes. Store in tightly covered container.

Per cookie: 26 calories
             .06 g fat
             25 mg sodium
             .80 mg cholesterol

●

Fake Rice Pudding

Yield: 2 servings

1 small package frozen cauliflower
Sugar substitute to taste
¼ cup skim milk
⅛ teaspoon **Indian Dessert Blend**
Dash of cinnamon

Cook cauliflower until extremely well done. Drain and mash or food process to a medium consistency. Add sweetener, Indian Dessert Blend, and milk. Place in custard cups and sprinkle with a light dash of cinnamon.

Per serving: 43 calories
             .36 g fat
             42 mg sodium
             .5 mg cholesterol

●

Skinny
Spices
Tip . . .

Try Tropical Whip for a light, elegant dessert: dissolve 1 package of artificially sweetened orange gelatin in 12 ounces of boiling ginger ale. Add 4 ounces cold orange juice and ⅛ teaspoon **Indian Dessert Blend**. Chill until just slightly thickened, then whip until fluffy. Spoon into 1-quart mold or individual molds. Chill until firm. Unmold and serve.

●

49.

Apple & Pumpkin Pie Blend

4 Tablespoons cinnamon

2 Tablespoons ground nutmeg

1 Tablespoon ground cloves

SPICY IDEAS

Bubbling Brown Sugar Peaches

Yield: 2 servings

4 fresh peaches
4 teaspoons brown sugar substitute
1 teaspoon **Apple & Pumpkin Pie Blend**

Skin, pit, and halve peaches. Sprinkle with brown sugar substitute and Apple & Pumpkin Pie Blend. Bake at 300° for 10 minutes, then put under broiler for a few minutes to brown slightly.

Per serving: 79 calories
.160 g fat
.5 mg sodium
.5 mg cholesterol

•

Berry Special
Yogurt Dessert
Yield: 2 servings

1 cup plain low-fat yogurt
½ cup strawberries
1½ teaspoon liquid sugar substitute
1 teaspoon vanilla
½ teaspoon **Apple & Pumpkin Pie Blend**

Combine all ingredients and chill thoroughly.
Per serving: 88 calories
1.9 g fat
80 mg sodium
.7 mg cholesterol

•

Skinny
Spices
Tip . . .

Sink your teeth into a Skinny Spices Cheese Danish. Toast one slice of 40-calorie bread lightly, and top with 2 ounces of low-fat cottage cheese. Sprinkle with **Apple & Pumpkin Pie Blend** and powdered or granular sugar substitute, and place under broiler for 3 to 4 minutes.

•

50.

Ginger Snap Blend

4 Tablespoons ground ginger

2 Tablespoons ground nutmeg

1 Tablespoon ground cloves

SPICY IDEAS

Holiday Pumpkin Custard

Yield: 4 servings

1 cup canned pumpkin
1 cup reconstituted dry non-fat milk
2 eggs
Liquid or powdered sweetener equal to ¼
    cup sugar
½ teaspoon vanilla
¾ teaspoon cinnamon
⅓ teaspoon **Ginger Snap Blend**

In large mixing bowl, beat all ingredients together until well blended. Pour into 4, 6-ounce custard cups and bake in preheated 350° oven 50 minutes or until knife inserted in center comes out clean.

Per serving: 85 calories
2.8 g fat;
65 mg sodium
108 mg cholesterol

●

Oriental Iced
Melon Balls
Yield: 6 servings

1 honeydew melon
2 Tablespoons lime juice
½ teaspoon **Ginger Snap Blend**

Ball honeydew melon, sprinkle with lime juice, and dust with Ginger Snap Blend. Serve ice cold.

Per serving: 82 calories
.24 g fat
.22 mg sodium
0 mg cholesterol

●

 Skinny
Spices
Tip . . .

For a change of pace at breakfast, try Skinny Spices French Toast. Soak 1 slice of 40-calorie bread in a well-beaten egg. Broil on foil. Sprinkle **Ginger Snap Blend** on top.

●

51.

Citrus Cooler Blend

•

4 Tablespoons Kool Aid Unsweetened Lemon Drink Mix

•

3 Tablespoons granulated sugar substitute

SPICY IDEAS

Dieter's Frozen Daiquiri
Yield: 1 serving

2 ounces lime juice
4 ounces water
1–2 teaspoons **Citrus Cooler Blend** to
taste
1 teaspoon rum extract

Blend above ingredients with ice in blender until slushy. Garnish with twist of lime or lemon and serve.

Per serving: 25 calories
.06 g fat
.46 mg sodium
0 mg cholesterol

•

●

Cherry Italian Ices
Yield: 1 large serving

3 ounces water
1 teaspoon Kool Aid unsweetened
cherry flavor
1 teaspoon **Citrus Cooler Blend**
Extra sweetener to taste
1–1½ cups crushed ice cubes

Mix all ingredients together and freeze until firm. Place
in blender for 30–45 seconds for slushy cherry Italian ices.
Per serving: 11 calories
0 g fat
0 mg sodium
0 mg cholesterol

●

 Skinny
Spices
Tip . . .

Experiment with individual spices that can add a new
dimension to sweet recipes: allspice, anise, cardamon, cinnamon, cloves, fennel, lemon peel, ginger, mace, nutmeg,
mint, orange peel, and rosemary.

●

Blah Busters: Brand-Name Substitutes for High-Calorie Foods

It's not surprising that most people think about dieting in terms of giving up their favorite foods. Bidding a fond farewell to pizza . . . sadly licking their last ice cream cone . . . skipping the creamy salad dressings . . . or tossing out the brownies. No wonder just the thought of dieting is enough to make you plunge head first into the refrigerator! Deprivation is the chief enemy of any dieter and can undermine even the most determined weight-loss effort.

It's been my experience that you stand a far better chance of being a successful dieter if you think *first* of the foods you love and then concentrate on finding lower-calorie substitutes that may be equally satisfying. (Then again, you may not find a good substitute, but at least you've become familiar with some of the alternatives.) Fortunately, more and more supermarkets are stocking healthier food choices, and dozens of new calorie-reduced products arrive on the shelves every day. What's more, food technology has improved to such a degree that most of these products successfully mimic their higher-calorie cousins and really can fool the taste buds.

Below are just some of the excellent brand-name, low-calorie substitutes that have helped me stay sane while fighting the battle of the bulge.

ALCOHOL

Instead of regular white wine at 80 calories per 4 ounces, try *Almaden Light Chablis* at 61 calories per 4 ounces.

Instead of regular rose wine at 88 calories per 4 ounces, try *Masson Light Premium Rose* at 64 calories per 4 ounces.

DAIRY ITEMS

Instead of regular butter or margarine at 100 calories per Tablespoon, try *Weight Watcher's Diet Margarine* in salted and unsalted varieties for 50 calories per Tablespoon.

Instead of diet margarine at 50 calories per Tablespoon, try *Butter Buds Sprinkles* at 4 calories per ½ teaspoon or *Weight Watcher's Butter-Flavored Spray* at 2 calories per spray.

Instead of Philadelphia Cream Cheese at 100 calories per ounce, try *Philadelphia Light* at 60 calories per ounce.

Instead of regular sour cream at 31 calories per Table-spoon, try *Molly McButter Sour Cream Sprinkles* at 8 calories per teaspoon.

Instead of Dannon regular Fruit Yogurt at 240 calories per cup, try *Dannon Light Yogurt* at 100 calories per cup.

Instead of regular half-and-half at 50 calories per Table-spoon, try *Non-Dairy Mocha Mix* at 20 calories per Tablespoon.

DESSERTS

Instead of regular high-butterfat, premium ice creams such as Haagen Dazs at 250–310 calories per 4 ounces, try *Simple Pleasures* ice cream in flavors like rum raisin, toffee crunch, chocolate, and strawberry at 110–140 per 3 ounces; or *Baskin Robbins Lite* in flavors like banana, chocolate mint, or jamoca almond at 110–130 calories per 4 ounces. For even fewer calories try *Baskin Robbins Sugar Free Ice Cream*, with only 80–100 calories per 4 ounces.

Instead of a regular brownie at 170 calories, try a *Weight Watcher's Brownie* at 100 calories.

Instead of regular cheesecake at 280 calories per slice, try *Weight Watcher's Strawberry Cheesecake* at 180 calories per slice, or *Weight Watcher's Brownie Cheesecake* at 200 calories per slice.

Instead of a regular slice of cinnamon Danish at 150 calories, try a slice of *Entemman's Light Cinnamon Twist* for 80 calories.

Instead of Reese's Peanut Butter Cups at 240 calories for 2, try *Weight Watcher's Frozen Peanut Butter Bars* at 60 calories per bar, or *Edy's Grand Light Peanut Butter and Chocolate Dairy Dessert* at 140 calories per 1/2 cup.

Instead of regular chocolate cupcakes at 170 calories each, try *Hostess Light Chocolate Cupcakes* at 110 calories each.

Instead of a slice of regular double-crust apple pie at 404 calories, try a *Weight Watcher's Apple Sweet Roll* at 190 calories.

Instead of Jello Regular Chocolate Pudding at 180 calories per 1/2 cup, try *Jello Sugar-Free Pudding* at 90 calories per 1/2 cup.

Instead of regular chocolate mousse at 754 calories per cup, try *Weight Watcher's Chocolate Flavor Mousse* at 120 calories per cup.

Instead of regular Extra Creamy Cool Whip for 14 calories per Tablespoon, try *Cool Whip Lite* at 8 calories per Tablespoon.

Instead of 2 regular oatmeal raisin cookies at 160 calories, try 2 *Entemman's Light Oatmeal Raisin Cookies* for 80 calories.

Instead of Jello Regular Gelatin at 80 calories per 1/2 cup, try *Jello Sugar-Free Gelatin* at 8 calories per 1/2 cup.

JAMS, JELLIES, SYRUPS, AND CONDIMENTS

Instead of regular ketchup at 18 calories per Tablespoon, try *Heinz Lite Ketchup* at 8 calories per Tablespoon.

Instead of regular jam at 18 calories per teaspoon, try *Smucker's Low Sugar Jams* at 8 calories per teaspoon.

Instead of regular Aunt Jemima Syrup at 110 calories per 2 Tablespoons, try *Aunt Jemima Lite* at 50 calories per 2 Tablespoons.

MAYONNAISE AND SALAD DRESSINGS

Instead of Kraft regular mayonnaise at 100 calories per Tablespoon, try *Kraft Light Reduced Calorie Mayonnaise* at 50 calories per Tablespoon.

Instead of regular ranch dressing at 50–60 calories per Tablespoon, try *Good Seasons Lite Ranch* at 30 calories per Tablespoon.

Instead of regular Italian dressing at 80 calories per Tablespoon, try *Kraft Oil Free Italian Dressing* at 4 calories per Tablespoon.

Instead of regular blue cheese dressing at 77 calories per Tablespoon, try *Wishbone Lite Chunky Blue Cheese* at 40 calories per Tablespoon.

MEAT, FISH, AND CHEESE

Instead of regular hot dogs at 150 calories per frank, try *Louis Rich Turkey Dogs* at 100 calories per frank.

Instead of regular tuna in oil at 150 calories per 2 ounces, try *Bumble Bee Solid White Tuna in Water* at 70 calories per 2 ounces.

Instead of regular cheese at 100 calories per slice, try *Weight Watcher's Cheese* at 50 calories per slice in American or sharp Cheddar; or *Lifetime Natural Cheese* in mild Cheddar, Monterey Jack, mozzarrella, Swiss, and Muenster at 50 calories per slice.

Instead of regular Kentucky Fried Chicken at 463 calories for a 2-piece snack dinner, try *Weight Watcher's Southern Fried Chicken Patty Dinner* at 340 calories.

Instead of regular beef stroganoff at 390 calories, try *Armour Classics Lite Beef Stroganoff* at 250 calories.

Instead of a regular Salisbury steak dinner at 500 calories, try *Healthy Choice Salisbury Steak Dinner* at 300 calories.

Instead of regular ham at 50 calories per slice, try *Louis Rich Turkey Ham* at 35 calories per slice.

Instead of regular bologna at 90 calories per slice, try *Louis Rich Turkey Bologna* at 60 calories per slice.

SNACKS

Instead of regular French bread sausage pizza at 840 calories, try *Lean Cuisine Sausage French Bread Pizza* at 330 calories.

Instead of 15 regular Doritos chips at 140 calories, try 15 *Doritos Lite* chips at 110 calories.

SOUPS, BOUILLONS, AND COCOAS

Instead of high-sodium chicken or beef bouillon at 90 mgs sodium, try *Herb Ox* chicken or beef bouillon packets wtih 5 mg sodium. The low- and high-sodium varieties both contain 8 calories.

Instead of regular cream of broccoli soup at 210 calories per 6 ounces, try *Lipton Lite Cup a Soup* at 40 calories per 6 ounces.

Instead of regular hot chocolate at 110 calories per 8 ounces, try *Carnation Sugar Free Hot Chocolate* at 50 calories per 8 ounces.

SUGAR AND BAKING INGREDIENTS

Instead of Pet Regular Evaporated Milk at 170 calories per ½ cup, try *Pet Light Evaporated Milk* at 100 calories per ½ cup.

Instead of regular brown sugar for 16 calories per teaspoon, try *Sugar Twin Brown Sugar Replacement* at 1½ calories per teaspoon.

Instead of regular white sugar for 10 calories per teaspoon, try *Equal®* for 4 calories per packet (equals 2 teaspoons of sugar); or 10 drops of any *liquid sweetener* at 0 calories per teaspoon.

Your Mail Order Guide to Spices

Although it's more convenient to buy your whole or ground spices locally, I know that not everyone's supermarket carries an extensive array of spices, and many people don't live near a gourmet store that carries some of the more exotic selections. The following catalog firms are reliable sources for mail order spices as well as for unusual condiments that can help add zip to any diet meal.

The Kitchen Shop
The Phoenix Building
670 Higuera Street
San Luis Obispo, CA 93401
(805) 541-0225

If for some reason I haven't been able to convince you by now that whipping up your own spice blends is fun and easy, you may want to cheat a little and send for a complete listing of Spice Hunter blends available through the Kitchen Shop of San Luis Obispo, California. These salt-free, sugar-free, all-natural spice blends come in delectable varieties such as Thai, Cajun/Creole, Fajita, Spicy Island Bean, Szechuan, and Pesto. The service at the Kitchen Shop is first-rate, and most spice blends cost just $2 to $4. Spice Hunter blends will even make your kitchen smell extra inviting when you're *not* cooking!

. . . .

Madeline's Gourmet Kitchen
P.O. Box 1302
Atascadero, CA 93423
(805) 461-4809

Here's another way to cheat if you don't want to mix up
Skinny Spices blends yourself. Madeline's offers a stagger-
ing variety of salt- and preservatives-free seasoning blends,
individual spices, and peppercorns. Plus, you'll receive a
free sample when you order the $1 catalog.

The Spice Merchant
P.O. Box 524
Jackson Hole, WY 83001
(307) 733-7811

This is my secret source for every Chinese, Japanese,
Thai, Indonesian, and Vietnamese condiment ever in-
vented, including the wasabi and dashi listed as ingredients
in the "Japanese Spice Blends" section. Be sure to try
owner Dave Bigge's special Sri Lanka Curry Kit for only
$4.50, with its pre-measured whole spices that you roast
and grind yourself to make a deliciously unusual curry
powder.

Mo Hotta Mo Betta
P.O. Box 4136
San Luis Obispo, CA 93403
(800) 462-3220 (nationwide)
(805) 544-4051 (in CA)

Husband and wife owners Tim and Wendy Eidson call
themselves hot and spicy gourmet extraordinaires, and
their 15-page catalog is mail order nirvana if you're the
kind of person who enjoys foods with a bite. Notable low-
calorie selections that I've used to spice up steamed
vegetables include Cajun Garlic Sauce, Jalapeño Mustard,
and Vinagré Picante, a blend of rice vinegar, chilies, garlic, tomatillos, and black pepper.

House of Spices
76-17 Broadway
Jackson Heights, NY 11373
(718) 476-1577

This homegrown catalog brings an Indian spice bazaar right to your doorstep. You'll find exotic spices such as fenugreek (mentioned in the "Indian Spice Blends" section), powdered fennel seeds, whole nutmeg, and sanchal (black salt) not to mention tongue twisters like calonji, methi barhdo, and pani puri masala.

G.B. Ratto & Company
821 Washington Street
Oakland, CA 94607
(800) 325-3483 (nationwide)
(800) 228-3515 (in CA)

A treasure-house of ethnic foods, Ratto's lets you choose among such unusual spice blends as berbere, a hot Ethiopian spice blend, and zather, a mixture of ground sumac and ground thyme that can be moistened with a touch of olive oil and slathered on diet bread for an authentic Mid-Eastern treat. My favorite spice is the powdered jalapeño peppers—a pinch can lend any dish a touch of Mexican magic. Ratto's also offers a marvelous selection of vinegars in hard-to-find flavors such as pear and orange sherry.

Spectacular Sauces
P.O. Box 30010
Alexandria, VA 22310
(800) 999-4949

Every unusual sauce, condiment, and salad dressing you could possibly imagine is listed in this exceptional, free catalog. Many are low in calories and fat and provide an easy way to liven up foods without spending any time in the kitchen. Especially noteworthy: Santa Fe Exotic's Pineapple Salsa; Nervous Nellie's Sweet Jalapeño Sauce, and Sengthongs' Thai Tamarind Dipping Sauce.

Dilijan Liquid Spice
Dilijan Products, Inc.
P.O. Box 145
Ringoes, NJ 08551
(201) 806-6048

This is a revolutionary new product—spices in liquid form with a two-year shelf life. Dilijan Liquid Spice is a one-to-one replacement for dried seasonings, but the flavor is absolutely garden-fresh. Available in Basil, Onion, Garlic, Dill, Chili, Hot Red Pepper, Oregano, Thyme, Curry, Clove, and Sage. The Basil is especially outstanding. All flavors are available by mail; send for their price list.

Seaside Banana Garden
6823 Santa Barbara Avenue
La Conchita, CA 93001
(805) 643-4061

Although Seaside is not a spice purveyor, I thought I'd include them here because bananas are the ultimate diet aid—low in calories, filling, and sweet. This is my favorite source for exotic bananas from all over the world. Call Seaside for prices on a 5½-lb. sampler pack of assorted varieties, all labeled so you get a "banana education" while you're enjoying their products.

Watkins
150 Liberty Street
Winona, MN 55987
(800) 533-8018

These are the famous flavor extract people, with varieties that taste sinful (like caramel and butter rum) but are just 1 or 2 calories per capful. Blend them into yogurt with a little sweetener or into ricotta cheese for a delightful taste treat.

San Francisco Herb Company
250 14th Street
San Francisco, CA 94103
(800) 227-4530

A free encyclopedic 32-page catalog full of tempting herbs and spices is available on request.

Dried Herbs from Nature's Wonderland
Penn Herb Company
603 N. 2nd Street
Philadelphia, PA 19123
(215) 925-3336

Stocks more than 500 herb varieties, teas, folk remedies, and books. And their catalog costs just $1.

The Herbfarm Armchair Sampler
32804 Issaquah-Fall City Road
Fall City, WA 98024
(206) 784-2222

The Herbfarm offers hundreds of herb varieties and herbal gifts through their 35-page catalog. In addition, the owners publish a bimonthly magazine called *The Herb Companion* for herb lovers, gardeners, and cooks for $21 a year. The catalog is free; a sample issue of the magazine costs $4.

Variety Spices
P.O. Box 277
Lithonia, GA 30058

Variety Spices specializes in out-of-the-ordinary spices and offers most of the unusual kinds mentioned in *Skinny Spices.* Their catalog costs $1, which is refundable on your first purchase.

More Spicy Reading

The following books were helpful in preparing *Skinny Spices* and inspirational in terms of my own weight loss.

Light & Spicy by Barbara Gibbons; Harper & Row, 1989. $10.95. "The Slim Gourmet" does it again with the most mouthwatering collection of spicy recipes anywhere. A true delight whether you're just browsing through, preparing a recipe, or sampling the delicious results.

The Nutri-System Flavor Set-Point Weight-Loss Cookbook by Susan S. Schiffman and Joan Scobey, with recipes by Robin Rifkin; Little, Brown, 1990. $18.95. You don't have to participate in the Nutri-System Program to benefit from this excellent combination of recipes and thought-provoking insights about dieting.

Chopstix by Hugh Carpenter and Terry Sandison; Stewart, Tabori & Chang, 1990. $29.95. A fun collection of low-fat, spicy recipes inspired by the enticing flavors of Asian and Mexican cuisine. **Chopstix** deliciously combines a cookbook, travel memoir, and visual tour of the Los Angeles contemporary art scene.

Microwave Gourmet Healthstyle Cookbook by Barbara Kafka; William Morrow & Co., 1989. $22.95. Great for dieters who want their food in a hurry and appreciate imaginative cooking with spices and herbs.

The Calorie Factor: The Dieter's Companion by Margo Feiden; Simon & Schuster, 1989. $29.95. A truly encyclopedic guide to calorie, fat, and carbohydrate listings for more than 250,000 foods. This is the only book I've ever found that even lists calorie counts for various types of sushi.

Delicious Diet Cookbook: The Sensible Way to Slim by Lois Levine; Macmillan Publishing, 1974. $6.95. Unfortunately, out of print, but a treasure trove of easy-to-fix low-cal goodies, with lots of good suggestions for enhancing food with the magic of herbs and spices.

Totally Hot: The Ultimate Hot Pepper Cookbook by Goodwin, Perry, and Wise; Dolphin/Doubleday, 1986. $12.95. Everything in this flame-red book is understandably hot and spicy, with many recipes for dieters who want to "go for the burn"—on their tongues, that is. This fine book is also out of print, but your local library may have a copy.

365 Diet Tips by Julie Davis; Ballantine Books, 1985. $3.50. A one-tip-a-day book filled with great advice for strengthening your resolve in the face of overwhelming temptation. Especially good as a source for developing moderate eating behaviors.

Diet Center It's a Natural Cookbook compiled by Sybil Ferguson; 1976. $3.00. Available only to Diet Center clients, this cookbook is filled with extremely low-calorie recipes that taste terrific. Try to borrow a copy from a program member, or look for one at a garage sale.

Sophie Kay's Yogurt Cookery by Sophie Kay; HP Books, 1978. $4.95. A healthy collection of yogurt-based recipes that even non-yogurt lovers will enjoy.

. . . .

New Gourmet Recipes for Dieters by Francine Prince, Simon & Schuster, 1981. $8.95. Fantastic heart-healthy recipes such as Banana Raisin Bars and Pink Panther Potatoes help keep dieters on track.

How to Lose Weight and Enjoy It by Lillian Dee and Marty Wolfson; Wolfson Publishing Co., 1972. $2.95. So old that it may actually qualify as an antique, this book touts a specific weight-loss program developed by the authors. Nevertheless, it contains some wonderful recipes (especially for salad dressings, dips, and desserts) that contain few or no calories.

The Free and Equal® Sweet Tooth Cookbook by Carole Krupa; Surrey Books, 1990. $8.95. All of Carol's books are marvelous, including this one, filled with easy-to-prepare recipes for sweets and desserts made with Equal® brand sugar substitute instead of sugar. Her companion volume, **The Free and Equal® Cookbook**, focuses on appetizers and main dishes made with Equal®. Both books are ideal for diabetics.